Daniel Jay Browne

The American bird fancier

Daniel Jay Browne

The American bird fancier

ISBN/EAN: 9783337147167

Printed in Europe, USA, Canada, Australia, Japan

Cover: Foto ©Lupo / pixelio.de

More available books at **www.hansebooks.com**

THE

AMERICAN BIRD FANCIER;

CONSIDERED WITH

REFERENCE TO THE BREEDING, REARING, FEEDING,
MANAGEMENT, AND PECULIARITIES

OF

CAGE AND HOUSE BIRDS;

WITH REMARKS ON THEIR

DISEASES AND REMEDIES;

DRAWN FROM AUTHENTIC SOURCES AND PERSONAL OBSERVATION.

BY D. J. BROWNE,

AUTHOR OF THE SYLVA AMERICANA, THE AMERICAN POULTRY YARD,
ETC., ETC.

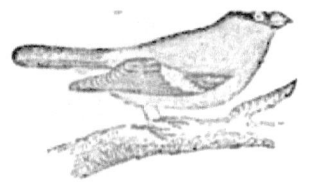

Illustrated with Engravings.

NEW-YORK:

ORANGE JUDD COMPANY,

245 BROADWAY.

1879.

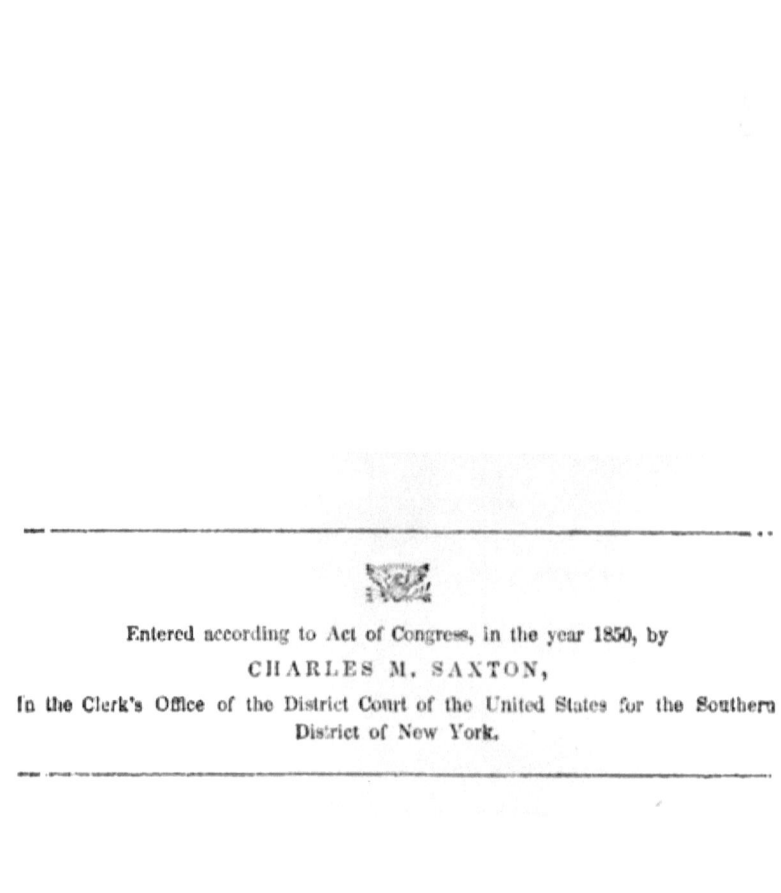

INDEX.

ILLUSTRATIONS.

ADVERTISEMENT.

IN issuing the present little treatise, the publisher would say a word respecting its character and the manner in which it has been composed. He is fully aware of the limited nature of the work, when compared with the boundless science of which it forms a part, and would have cheerfully extended the subject had he believed the wants and economy of the American public required it. To those who wish further to pursue the subject, he would recommend the more elaborate treatises of Audubon, Wilson, Bonaparte, Nuttall, and Dekay, for American birds, and particularly the works of Dr. Bechstein for the birds of Europe.

An intimate knowledge of Natural History, being an enthusiastic lover of the feathered tribes, having been familiar with them from his earliest childhood, has well qualified Mr. Browne for writing this, and if necessary, an extensive work. He will doubtless be recollected by many as the editor of " The Naturalist," a monthly periodical, published in Boston some twenty years ago, and more recently as the author of the " American Poultry Yard " and of a treatise on American trees Within the above-named period, he has travelled and resided for a considerable time in various parts of North and South America, the West Indies, Europe, and Western Africa, (having passed several months at the Canary Islands,) for the express purpose of investigating, among other objects, the natural features of those countries, where he had ample opportunities for studying the habits of birds both in a state of nature, and in confinement, the most advantageous means of procuring them, and the proper mode of feeding and maintaining them in health.

In order that the author may not be accused of the reproach of wearing " borrowed plumes," it is hereby candidly confessed that he has made a free use of the writings of Audubon, Nuttall, and particularly those of Dr. Bechstein, as well as of the " Boy's Treasury of Sports," without giving them, in numerous instances, such credit as the punctilious critic would seem to demand. Be this as it may, the author has endeavored not to deviate from established custom, except in cases where he deemed it expedient to change the language, in part, for the sake of brevity, elucidation, or *Americanising* the subject, or adapting it to our climate, economy, and social condition. Much of the matter, however, and several of the illustrations, he claims to be original.

The publisher, therefore, confidently presents the " American Bird Fancier " to the public with the full belief that it containes such information on the subject, as the taste and economy of our fair country women and their children require.

C. M. SAXTON.

NEW YORK, *March 20*, 1850.

INTRODUCTION

IRDS, from their elegant and beautiful coloring, the graceful ease of their flight, their varied music, their tender solicitude for their young, their singular and engaging instincts, their susceptibility of domestication, and their subserviency to the sustenance of man, have, for ages past, attracted universal admiration, and, as objects of human interest, and even affection, they stand foremost, perhaps, in the entire range of animated nature.

The structure of birds and their habits of life, are wonderfully adapted to the various functions they are destined to perform. The pointed beak, the long and pliant neck, the gently-swelling shoulder, the expansive wings, the tapering tail, the light and bony feet, are all wisely calculated to assist and accelerate their motion through the yielding air. Every part of their frame is formed for lightness and buoyancy; their bodies are covered with a soft and delicate plumage, so disposed as to protect them from the intense cold of the atmosphere through which they pass; their wings are made of the lightest materials, and yet, the force with which they strike the air is so great, as to impel their bodies forward with astonishing rapidity, while the tail serves as a rudder to direct them to the different objects of their pursuit.

The internal structure of birds is no less wisely adapted to the same purposes. Their lungs have several openings, communicating with corresponding air bags, or cells, which fill the whole cavity of the body from the neck downwards, and into which the air passes and re-passes, in the process of breathing. This is not all; their very bones are hollowed out with the design of receiving air from the lungs, from which air pipes are conveyed to the most solid parts of the body, and even into the quills and plumelets of the feathers which are hollow or spongy for its reception. As all these hollow parts, as well as the cells, are only open on the side communicating with the lungs, the bird requires only to take in a full breath to fill and distend its whole body with air, which, in consequence of the considerable heat of its body, is rendered much lighter than the air of the atmosphere. By forcing this air out of the body again, the weight becomes so much increased, that birds of a large size can dart down from great heights in the air with astonishing rapidity.

This almost universal diffusion of air in the bodies of birds is of infinite use to them, not only in these long and laborious flights, but likewise in preventing their respiration from being stopped or interrupted by the rapidity of their motion through a resisting medium. Were it possible for man to move with the swiftness of a swallow, the actual resistance of the air as he is not provided with internal reservoirs similar to those of birds, would soon suffocate him

The digestive organs of birds form them into two distinct natural classes; those with cartilaginous stomachs, covered with very strong muscles, called a *gizzard*; and those with membranous stomachs more resembling those of carnivorous quadrupeds. The former is given to birds, the principal food of which is grain and seeds of various kinds, or other hard substances that require much friction to divide, or comminute, to assist which, gravel is necessary; the latter is given to birds which feed upon flesh or fish, and whose digestion is accelerated more by the gastric juice than by the action of the stomach. Those of the first class digest or retain every substance swallowed; and those which eject or disgorge innutritious matter unavoidably taken in, such as feathers, fur, bones, &c., belong to the second class, as is conspicuous in those that feed on fish. Graminivorous birds seem to possess the power of retaining the small stones taken into the gizzard, or evacuating them, when they become polished and less useful, but cannot disgorge them. In a state of nature, the quantity of gravel taken in, must be regulated, no doubt, by the sensation of the stomach; but, wonderful as it may seem, in domesticated animals, those instinctive faculties are deranged. Instances frequently occur where the whole cavity of the gizzard is filled with gravel stones. The food of graminivorous birds is conveyed entire into the first stomach, or craw, where it undergoes a partial dilution by a liquor secreted from the glands, and spread over its surface. It is then received into another species of stomach, where it is still further diluted, after which it is transmitted into the gizzard, or true stomach, consisting of two very strong muscles, externally covered with a tendinous substance, and lined with a thick membrane of prodigious power and strength, in which organ the food is completely triturated, and prepared for the operation of the gastric juices.

Graminivorous birds partake much of the nature and disposition of herbivorous quadrupeds, agreeing with them in the number of their stomachs, the quality of their food, and the gentleness of their manners. Content with the seeds of plants, with fruits, insects, and worms, their principal attention is directed to procuring food, hatching and rearing their offspring, and eluding the snares of men and the attacks of predaceous animals. The stomachs of carnivorous birds are smaller than those of the graminivorous kinds, and their intestines are much shorter. Many species of birds possess a reservoir for food, called a *craw*, or *crop*, which seems to answer the same purpose as the first stomach of ruminating animals. Here it is that the food is softened and prepared for the stomach, or carried to the young.

THE SONG OF BIRDS.

THE song of birds is always, if not the expression of love, at least that of pleasure. Thus, the nightingale sings only as long as pairing time or hatching lasts, and is silent as soon as it is compelled to feed its young; whereas, the goldfinch and Canary sing throughout the year, and only cease when moulting dejects them. The continuation of the song of these birds, however, by no means proves that it is not occasioned by the stimulus of love.

Song appears to be the especial privilege of the male, whereby it either attracts the female or seeks to obtain her love; for there are but few females which produce notes similar to the song of the male, and these almost exclusively in a state of widowhood. They listen attentively, in fact, to the greater or less perfection or charm of the song of the male, to bestow upon that one their love whom they esteem the most accomplished singer. Thus, the most sprightly hen Canary selects the best singer; and the chaffinch, when at liberty, will choose from among a hundred males the one whose song best pleases **her**.

HABITATION OF CAGE OR CHAMBER BIRDS.

Birds which are kept only on account of their beauty, or for their animation and vivacity, are generally kept best in a room where they can run or fly freely about, and where they can resort at night for repose, to a large cage of many compartments, or to one or more fir trees. But larger birds should have an apartment expressly appropriated to them, as their fæces smell unpleasantly in a dwelling room, whence also they require constant cleaning. Smaller birds may be allowed to run freely about, having a small tree or a cage hung up for them to roost in. With this degree of liberty, many birds sing better than when confined in a cage.

Cleanliness is in every respect very important in keeping birds, for they are not only thereby preserved for many years but it keeps them constantly healthy and cheerful; hence it is necessary that the cage should be cleaned at least once a-week, and birds which run about upon the ground, should have the sand renewed frequently; the perches also of such as use them should be carefully cleaned. If this be not attended to, the birds will become sickly, and will suffer from lame feet, gout, and other maladies, terminating in the loss of their toes, as all must have experienced who have been accustomed to keep birds, and have neglected cleansing them. In cleaning their feet, it is very requisite that the bird should have them dipped in water before the dirt is removed; for if this be not done, the skin, to which the dirt closely adheres, comes off with it, which renders the bird not merely lame, but also attracts to the part all the unhealthy humors generated by their unnatural mode of living.

It is in the feet indeed that cage or chamber birds chiefly suffer, and they must be daily examined to see that nothing gets entangled about them, as hair thus twisted will frequently cut very deep, and in the course of a few days, that portion of the foot or toe, so tied up, will dry up and fall off. Very great

attention must be paid to this particular circumstance, as
scarcely a bird can be preserved for any length of time with
all its toes uninjured. It is not to be denied, however, that
many birds keep themselves exceedingly neat, whilst others,
even of the same genus, are so uncleanly, that they are not
only always soiling themselves, but never clean their feet,
beak, nor wings.

Some bird fanciers take delight in making birds so tame as
to be taken upon the hand into the open air, or to be allowed
to fly away and come back again upon a call. "One of my
friends," says Dr. Bechstein, "who has tamed birds as well as
otters, adders, foxes, weasels, and martins, so that they would
follow him upon a sign given, adopts the following easy and
certain method to effect it:—When he wishes to accustom a
bird to fly abroad, or to go out with him perched upon his
finger or his shoulder, he first teases it with a soft feather in
its cage which stands open. The bird soon snaps at the feather,
and then at his finger, and it will then come out of the cage, and
perch upon the extended finger; he immediately strokes it,
and lays a few choice morsels before it. These, the bird will
soon take out of the hand itself. He then commences by
familiarising the bird with some peculiar call or whistle, and
he carries it, as soon as it permits itself to be grasped in the
hand, placed upon his hand or shoulder, from chamber to
chamber, taking care to close the doors and windows; he then
suffers it to fly, and calls it back again. As soon as it attends
to this call without being scared or frightened, he takes it
cautiously into the open air, and thus the bird becomes
gradually so accustomed to him that he can carry it abroad or
into company without its offering to fly away."

Care, however, must be taken not to carry adult birds, which
have been thus tamed, into the open air where they can hear
their fellows, in the spring or at pairing time, which are
usually the periods when they show indications of resuming
their native wildness.

If it is wished to teach a bird to eat out of the mouth, it
must be kept for a time in the cage without food, and then

when sitting upon the finger its favorite food must be held to
it upon the tip of the exteded tongue. Hunger soon teaches it
to peck. Such tame birds learn, also, speedily to sing upon the
finger. To accomplisL this, nothing more is necessary than
to induce it by certain tones, motions, and fondling. But it
is still further requisite to observe in this process of taming,
that, to be effectual, it should be continued for a longer time
than is here laid down. May we not presume that the bird
will, in the course of a few weeks, do that freely which has
been taught, or rather forced upon it, in this short space of
time.

FOOD OF TAME BIRDS.

In selecting the food of birds in confinement, it is requisite
to do so, as far as is practicable, in accordance with the nature
of its food in a natural state. This, indeed, is frequently
difficult, if not wholly impossible. Great caution, therefore,
must be observed to accustom the birds we keep, or rather
their stomachs, by degrees, to the food we are compelled to
supply them, although it cannot be denied that there are
birds, also, which, as soon as they are placed in the aviary, eat
anything that is given to them. But others are more delicate, and will not eat at all, partly from grief at the loss of
their liberty, and partly from not finding the food they have
been accustomed to. Great care must therefore, be taken of
these. If such as are known to be delicate—the majority of
singing birds—for instance, commence greedily eating as soon
as they are placed in the chamber, it is a bad sign; for they
will certainly die, as it implies an unnatural indifference to the
loss of their liberty, which is almost always deducible from
sickliness. Those which creep into corners and seem for
some hours to pine, it is less necessary to be anxious
about; but they must not be disturbed until their ill-humor
subsides.

Dr. Meyer, of Offenbach, Germany, remarks as follows upon

this subject :—'An almost unfailing mode of accustoming birds to their food, which is known to be extremely difficult in many, is thus: Let the bird be placed in a cage in the room where it is purposed to be kept; give it freely appropriate food and drink in open vessels; leave it thus undisturbed for several hours; then catch it and dip it in fresh water, and again place it in its former cage. It will now sit for some moments thoroughly exhausted, but will soon recover and begin preening itself, and in the course of a few minutes become extremely animated, and then it will certainly eat the food put before it. Doubtless the same cause produces an appetite in birds after bathing as in man."

In order to give some general rules for the best food of cage or house birds, I have divided them, after Dr. Bechstein, into four following classes :—

The first comprehends those birds which live only on seeds, such as Canaries, goldfinches, Siskins, &c.

The second are those which feed both on seeds and insects, such as quails, larks, cat birds, and mocking birds; some of these also eat the buds and berries of trees.

The third are those which seek only berries and insects, such as nightingales, redbreasts, thrushes, and the like.

The fourth are those which eat insects only, such as wagtails, woodpeckers, cuckoos, &c.

The birds in the last-named class are the most difficult to preserve; but most of them, having nothing particular in their song, offer but little compensation for the trouble and care which they require.

RECIPE FOR A GENERAL FOOD.—In proportion to the number of birds, white bread enough must be baked to last for three months. When it is well baked and stale, it must be put again into the oven, and left there until cold. It is then fit to be pounded in a mortar, and will keep several months without becoming bad. Every day a teaspoonful for each bird is taken of this meal, on which is poured three times as much cold, or lukewarm, (but not boiling,) milk. If the meal be good, a firm paste will be formed, which must be chopped very small on a board. This paste, which is very nourishing, may be kept a long time without becoming sour or sticky; on the contrary, it is always dry and brittle. As soon as a delicate bird is brought in, some flies or chopped worms should be mixed with the paste, which will attract it to eat. It will soon be accustomed to this food, which will keep it in life and health.

Although the notice of a universal remedy is generally suspicious, the two following sorts of paste have been recommended, and used with success, agreeing well with all, or nearly all, tamed birds, if we except those which are confined in cages on account of their beautiful songs. They are not only very simple and cheap, but also prevent great loss of time to those who possess a great number of birds.

UNIVERSAL PASTE.—To make the first paste, take a white loaf which is well baked and stale; put it into fresh water, and leave it there until quite soaked through; then squeeze out the water and pour boiled milk over the loaf, adding about two thirds the quantity of barley meal with the bran well sifted out, or, what is still better, wheat meal.

For the second paste, grate a carrot very nicely (this root may be kept nearly a whole year if buried in sand); then soak a small white loaf in fresh water, press the water out, and put it and the grated carrot into an earthen pan; add two handfuls of barley or wheat meal, and mix the whole well together with a pestle.

These pastes should be made fresh every morning, as they soon become sour, particularly the first, and consequently hurtful.

Every morning, fresh water must be given to the birds, both for drinking and bathing. When a great many are left at liberty, one dish will do for them all, about eight inches long, and two in width and depth, divided into several partitions, by which means they are prevented from plunging entirely into the water, and in consequence making the place always dirty and damp. A vessel of the same size and shape will do for holding the universal paste, but then it must have no partitions.

Those birds which devour everything thrown to them, must be protected against the possibility of having any food given to them that contains pepper or much salt, and especially against putrid meat. This is a universal rule of precaution. It may further be observed, that to birds confined in cages, no more must be given than they can eat during the day otherwise they will accustom themselves to scatter their food out of the vessel, and eat the best first, leaving the worst for subsequent fare; and are consequently to-day well, and drooping to-morrow.

BREEDING.

THERE is but little to be said of the breeding of birds in confinement, as, in the majority of cases, it is difficult to accomplish, excepting in such as can be thoroughly familiarised, like Canaries. Of breeding places, there are two kinds, one a large cage made of wire or wood, and the other the entire range of a room. Both should be dry, airy, and exposed in our northern climate to the warmth and light of the sun. It is chiefly requisite to supply birds that are to breed with a still, solitary, and spacious abode; and it is preferable to give them an entire apartment in which evergreens are placed that have not lost their leaves. Above all things, it is desirable to make this abode as nearly resemble their natural dwelling place as possible, that they may be excited to pair. With every care, however, to render their breeding place like the natural one, it is difficult to supply them with the necessary materials for their nests. This deficiency should be supplied by nests artificially formed of woven cotton, willow, straw, or turned wood, into which they will only have to convey appropriate linings; for this purpose, they must be supplied with the hair of animals and raw silk, cotton, wool, &c.

Especial care must be taken to furnish the birds with requisite food, which partly contributes to fit old ones for breeding, and which must also be suited to the varying ages of the reared young. In this particular, I shall mention what must be done, in the articles relating to the different species described in the subsequent part of this work.

BREEDING CAGE.

TIME FOR REMOVING WILD BIRDS FROM THE NEST.

It may be necessary that I should give some general directions about the time at which it is desirable to remove young wild birds, intended to be reared, from the nest. This is when the tail quills shoot forth, and when all the feathers begin to expand, and before the birds can yet completely open their eyes. If they are removed earlier, their stomachs are too weak to endure the food of the aviary, and if it take place later, it is usually extremely difficult to induce them to open their beaks to receive food with which they are unacquainted. But there are species of birds which can at all times be easily fed and tamed. As a general rule, all seed-eating birds may be tamed, both adult and young.

DISEASES OF TAME BIRDS.

Like all tame animals, birds that are kept in confinement, are exposed to more maladies than those which live at large;[*] and especially as they are frequently so closely confined in cages that they have scarcely room to move. These maladies, however, are considerably increased by their having all kinds of delicacies, as pastry, sugar, &c., given them, which spoil their stomachs and usually produce a slow consumption.

The following are the chief maladies which affect birds, and their remedies, as laid down by Dr. Bechstein, the efficiency of which he proved upon his own. Indeed, the variety of birds, as well as the variety of their food, requires also a difference of treatment in their maladies; and in speaking of each species, I shall have occasion to notice how their peculiar diseases may be treated, when the general remedies are not suitable to their nature.

[*] It has been frequently asserted that birds in their natural state are never ill, but this is unfounded.

Pip, or Thrush.—This is a catarrh, or cold, by which the nostrils are stopped up, and the membrane covering the tongue is hardened by inflammation. In large birds, it is common to remove this skin, taking it off from the base to the tip; but rough modes should not be used for doing it. A little borax, dissolved in water, may be applied to the tongue with a camel-hair pencil two or three times a-day until a healthy action is produced. By this means, this part can again perspire, the saliva necessary for digestion can flow, and the taste and appetite return. A mixture of fresh butter, pepper, and garlic, generally cures this catarrh. It is a good thing, also, for the birds to drink the pectoral infusion of speedwell (*Veronica officinalis*); and the nostrils may be opened by passing up a small feather dipped in oil. The ruffling of the head, the beak often open and yellow at its base, and the tongue dry, are the most decisive indications of this disease.

Rheum.—The symptoms of this disease are frequent sneezing and shaking of the head. Some drops of pectoral elixir in the infusion of speedwell, which the sick birds must be made to take, appears to be the most efficacious remedy.

When it is merely hoarseness, Dr. Handel, of Mentz, in France, gave to his birds for several days, as their only drink, a very dilute decoction of dry figs, sweetened with a little sugar, and afterwards purged them, for two days following, with the juice of carrots.

Asthma.—This is a very common disease among house birds. Those attacked with it have their breath short, often open their beaks as if to gasp for more air, and, when agitated or frightened, keep them open for a long time.

The cause of this disease may doubtless be found in the mode of life which the birds lead. Their food is generally too dry and heating, being principally hemp seed, which is very injurious, but liked by all; and is the more hurtful, as it inclines them to eat too much. If to this, be added the unchanged air of the rooms, particularly those which have stoves instead of chimneys, and the great heat which is kept up during winter, it is plain that there is much to injure the delicate lungs of the birds.

A moist and refreshing regimen and some aperients, more or less often, according to the violence of the disease, appears the most appropriate remedy. A favorite linnet and goldfinch, mentioned by Dr. Bechstein, when attacked with very bad asthma, were relieved and preserved for several years by the following method :—

The first thing was to leave off hemp seed entirely, confining them solely to rape seed; but giving them at the same time an abundance of bread, soaked in pure water, and then pressed; lettuce, endive, or water cresses, according to the season, twice a-week, giving them bread boiled in milk, about the size of a nutmeg. This is made by throwing a piece of the crumb of white bread, about the size of a nut, into a teacupful of milk, boiling it, and stirring it all the time with a wooden spoon till it is of the consistency of pap. It must be quite cold before it is given to the birds, and must always be made fresh, for if sour, it will prove injurious.

This paste, which they are very fond of, purges them sufficiently, and sensibly relieves them. In very violent attacks, nothing but this paste ought to be given for two or three days following, and this will soon give the desired relief.

When the disease is slight, or only begun, it is sufficient to give the bread and milk once in three or four days. When employed under similar circumstances, this treatment has cured several very valuable birds. It may not be useless here to renew the advice of always giving the birds an opportunity of bathing every day, by putting in their way a saucer, or any other small shallow bath, filled with water, which should never be too cold, and in winter always milkwarm.

One thing which is very injurious to the lungs of birds, and which too often occurs, is the fright occasioned by tormenting them, or by seizing them too suddenly; for the poor little things often rupture a blood vessel in the breast while beating themselves about. A drop of blood in the beak is the sign, and a speedy death is the general consequence. If this do not happen, the breathing is not the less difficult and painful; and recovery is rare, at least without the greatest care and attention.

Birds that eat insects and worms, occasionally, by accident, swallow some extraneous substance, which, sticking in their throat, stops their respiration and stifles them. The only remedy is to extract the foreign body, which requires much skill and dexterity.

When asthma is brought on by eating seeds, which are too old, spoiled, or rancid, Dr. Handel recommends some drops of oxymel, (honey and vinegar boiled to a syrup,) to be swallowed for eight days following. But the best way is to change the seed, and be sure there is none but good seed in the feeding trough.

ATROPHY, OR WASTING.—This is caused by giving unnatural food to the bird, which destroys the digestive power of its stomach. In this case, it disgorges its food, ruffles its feathers, and does not arrange them, and becomes thin very fast. The best thing is to make it swallow a common spider, which purges it, and put a rusty nail into its water, which strengthens the tone of the stomach, giving it at the same time its proper and natural food. Green food, such as lettuce, endive, chickweed, and particularly water cresses, is the safest remedy. A very great appetite is a sign of this disease. A Siskin, mentioned by Dr. Bechstein, that was dying of atrophy, had nothing but water cresses for three days following, and on the fourth he sung.

CONSUMPTION.—This is usually the result of unnatural food, which interrupts the function of digestion, and it is recognised by the bird inflating and distending itself. The feathers are ruffled, and the flesh dwindles. No better remedy, perhaps, can be found than to give such birds a common spider, which purges them, and to lay in their water a rusty nail, which strengthens the stomach. They must, at the same time, be fed with the best description of their appropriate food. In birds which will eat vegetables, and especially water cresses, this will be found the surest remedy against consumption, or waste. Usually, birds suffering from this malady have a voracious appetite for green food. Dr. Bechstein fed a Siskin, which had already completely wasted, for three successive days, with nothing but water cresses, and on the fourth it recommenced singing.

Costiveness.—This disease may be discovered from the frequent unsuccessful endeavors of the bird to relieve itself. Aperients will be of use. If a spider does not produce the desired effect, anoint the vent of the bird with the head of a pin steeped in linseed oil; this sort of clyster generally succeeds. Boiled bread and milk is also of great service.

Diarrhœa.—This is a disease to which birds that have been caught recently are very subject, before they are accustomed to their new food. Most of these die of it; they continually void a white calcareous matter, which sticks to the feathers round the vent, and being very acrid causes inflammation in that part and in the intestines. Sometimes chalybeate water, (iron water,) and the oil clyster produce good effects; but it is better, if possible, to procure for the bird its most natural food. Some people pull out the feathers from the tail and vent, and then rub these parts with fresh butter, but this is a very painful and cruel operation. They also mix the yolk of an egg boiled very hard with their food, but this does not succeed very well. If there be any hope of curing this disease, it is by attacking it at the beginning, before inflammation is violent; boiled bread and milk, a plenty of lettuce, or any other similar green refreshing food, generally effects a cure.

In a case of chronic diarrhœa, which almost reduces the birds to skeletons, Dr. Handel, of France, prescribes chalybeate water, mixed with a little milk for their drink, which, he says, is an easy and certain cure.

Bloody Flux.—This is a disease with which some parrots are attacked. The best remedy is to make the birds drink a plenty of boiled milk, or even very fat broth; for their intestines, which are very much irritated, require something soothing to protect them from the acrid discharges, which, at the same time, must by corrected be healing food. Birds in this state, generally do nothing but drink; therefore plenty of boiled milk should be given them, as it nourishes them, as well as acts medicinally, but should it appear to turn sour in the stomach, it must, at least for some time, be discontinued.

OBSTRUCTION OF THE RUMP GLAND.—This gland, which is on the rump, and contains the oil employed for anointing the feathers, sometimes becomes hard and inflamed, and an abscess forms there. In this case, the bird often pierces it itself, or it may be softened by applying fresh butter without any salt; but it is better to use an ointment made of white lead, litharge, wax, and olive oil, which may be had of any good chemist or apothecary. The general method is to pierce or cut the hardened gland, in order to let out the matter.

The gland is known to be obstructed when the feathers, which surround it, are ruffled, the bird never ceasing to peck them, and instead of being yellow it becomes brown. Dr. Bechstein says, this disease is very rare among wild birds, for, being exposed to damp, and bathing often, they make more use of the liquor in the gland, consequently, it does not accumulate sufficiently to become corrupted, sour, or cancerous. This confirms the necessity of giving them the means of bathing as often as instinct would induce them, as nothing can be more favorable to their health.

Dr. Handel, after piercing the gland, recommends a little magnesia to be mixed with the bird's drink.

EPILEPSY.—This is a disease with which house birds are very often attacked. What has been found to be most useful in this case, is to plunge the sick birds every now and then into very cold water, letting them fall suddenly into it, and cutting their claws, or at least one or two, short enough for the blood to run.

From bleeding giving so much relief, one would think that this disease is a kind of apoplexy, occasioned by want of exercise and too much food. Bullfinches and thrushes are more subject to it than any other birds, and bleeding always cures them, which has been done with great success in the following manner, but much delicacy and skill are required, as there would be great danger of laming the bird:—A very small hole is made on the surface of the claw, with a lancet or very sharp penknife; it is then plunged in lukewarm water, and if the operation be well done, the blood runs like a thread of red silk; when removed from the water, the bleeding stops; no bandage nor dressing is required.

TYMPANY OR BLOATING.—In this disorder, the skin on one part of the body, or even the whole body, rises and swells to so great a degree that it is stretched like a drum. It is generally sufficient to pierce it with a pin, so as to let the air escape, and the bird will be cured.

DISEASE IN THE FEET.—House birds are often subject to bad feet. From the second year, they become pale, and lose their freshness. They must be frequently cleaned, taking care to remove the skin; the thick loose scales ought also to be taken off, but with all possible precaution.

The gout occasions the feet to swell; they are also so scaly and painful that the poor little bird cannot support itself without resting on the points of its wings. Dr. Handel prescribes a warm fomentation with a decoction of soapwort (*Saponaria officinalis*). If a foot should be bruised or broken, he advises that the diseased bird should be shut up in a very small cage, the bottom of which is very smooth and even, without any perches, or anything which would tempt it to hop, and put in a very quiet and solitary place, out of the way of anything which might produce agitation. In this manner, the bird will cure itself in a little time, without any bandage or plaster of any kind.

Dr. Bechstein was of the opinion that the principal cause of bad feet is want of bathing. The scales, contracting from dryness, occasion great pain; in order to remove them with ease, and without danger, the feet must be softened in lukewarm water. The following method has been used with a bullfinch with success:—Its cage was made with a movable tin bottom, which, being half or three quarters of an inch deep, could hold water, that was put in tepid, to bathe the bird;

the perches were then removed, so that the bird was obliged to remain in the water, where it was left for half an hour, sometimes throwing it hemp seed to amuse it. After repeating the bath once or twice, the bird became very fond of it; and it was remarked that its feet became, if we may say so, quite young again. The scales being sufficiently softened, the middle of each was cut lengthwise without reaching the flesh; this made the sides easily fall off. It is better to remove only two scales a-day, that the bird may not be wearied. By continuing the bath three times a-week, the feet become healthy and supple, and the bird is easy.

Sore Eyes.—The juice of red beet for drink, and also as a liniment, greatly relieves this disorder. Dr. Handel, of Mentz, recommends washing the eyes, when disposed to blindness, with an infusion of the root of white hellebore.

Tumors and Ulcers.—As to the tumors and ulcers which come on the heads of the birds, Dr. Handel touches them with a middling-sized red-hot knitting needle. This makes the watery humor run out, and the wound afterwards dries and heals. To soften the pain, a little liquid black soap is used. If, from the softness of the tumor, matter seems to have formed, it should be rubbed with fresh butter until it is come to a head; it may then be emptied, and opened by a few drops of essence of myrrh. During all this time, the bird must have nothing but beet juice to drink.

Ulcers in the palate and throat may be cured by making the bird drink the milk of almonds for several days, at the same time lightly touching the ulcers several times a-day with a feather dipped in a mixture of honey and borax.

Moulting.—This occurrence, though natural, is generally accompanied with disease, during which the birds ought to be taken great care of. Their food should be changed, but without giving any heating delicacies, which are very injurious.

It has been observed that birds always moult at the time when their food is most abundant; the forest birds may then be seen approaching fields and cultivated places, where, having plenty of insects and seeds, they cannot suffer from want;

indeed, the loss of their feathers prevents their taking long flights, and the reproduction of them occasions a loss of flesh which must be repaired. An abundance of food is therefore necessary, and, following this rule, during moulting, some additional food must be given to house birds, appropriate to the different species—millet or Canary seed, a little hemp seed, white bread soaked in water, and lettuce, or endive, to those which feed on seeds; with a few more worms and ants' eggs to those that eat insects; all should have bread soaked in boiled milk, warmth, and baths. Nothing has succeeded better than this regimen.

VERTIGO, OR GIDDINESS.—This, without being properly a disease, is rather common, and is occasioned by the trick which the birds of the first class have, of turning their head and neck so far round that they fall off their perch. They may be easily cured of this trick by throwing a covering over the top of the cage, which prevents their seeing anything above them, for it is with looking up that this *giddiness* comes on.

PAIRING FEVER.—A disease which may be called the " pairing fever" must not be forgotten here. House birds are usually attacked with it in the spring, or at the time when the inclination to pair is greatest. They cease to sing, become sorrowful and thin, ruffle their feathers, and die. This fever generally first seizes those which are confined in cages; it appears to arise from their mode of life, which is too uniform and wearying. They may be cured merely by placing them in the window, where they are soon so much refreshed that they forget their grief, their desire for liberty, or for pairing, and resume their liveliness and song.

It has been observed that a single female in the room is sufficient to cause this disease to all the males of the same family, though of different species. Removing the female will cure them directly. The males and females, at this season, must be separated, so that they cannot see nor hear one another. This, perhaps, is the reason that a male, when put in the window, is soon cured.

PARASITIC VERMIN.—If birds are sometimes restless, especially of a night, and if they are observed to be frequently feeling with their beaks about the abdomen, back, or wings, they must be examined to see if no small yellow insects, (lice or mites,) may be discovered upon the body, or between the feathers. If this be the case, they must be sprinkled by means of a small syringe with water, in which quicksilver has been steeped, or with a much diluted infusion of tobacco, for several successive days, whereby these vermin are destroyed or chased away. Another mode of getting rid of the lice is to bathe the birds frequently, and to give them, daily, fresh or dry sand, and to be very particular in keeping them exceedingly clean.

Unnatural Fatness.—If it be found that the birds become unnaturally fat, which is often the case, especially during autumn, in some species of warblers, their too nutritious food must be changed and Swedish turnips, (ruta-bagas,) be mixed in it, and dry ants' eggs put into their drink, which much checks their corpulency.

THE CANARY BIRD.

Synonymes.

Fringilla canaria, ...	Of Ornithologists.
Serin de Canarie, ...	Of the French.
Canarienvogel, ...	Of the Germans.
Canario, ...	Of the Spaniards and Portuguese.
Canarino, ...	Of the Italians.
Canary Bird, Canary, ...	Of the British and Anglo-Americans.

THE Canary bird, from its beautiful plumage, elegant shape, singular capacity, and attractive familiarity, as well as from the charms and melodies with which it enlivens our rooms, has always been agreeable to the fancier, and may, emphatically be called the *real* "cage bird." Some of them we find melancholy, others cheerful; some angry, others peaceful; some intelligent, others dull; some industrious, others idle; some greedy, others frugal. But they have chiefly made themselves beloved by their animated, powerful, and varied song, which lasts almost throughout the whole year, and with some even during the time of moulting.

These birds are also distinguished by their correctness of ear, the remarkable skill they possess of imitating all tones, and their excellent memory. Not only do they imitate the notes of other birds, which they greatly improve by mixing them with their own, but they will even learn to utter short words with some degree of correctness. In their wild and undomesticated state, their song is unvaried, as with most other birds, less melodious, of fewer notes, and uttered at longer intervals than with us; at least, I found them so, as far as my observation extended, when a resident of the Canary Isles.

ORIGIN AND HISTORY.

THOSE birds, from which are descended the Canaries now kept and reared throughout the whole of Europe, and even in Russia and Siberia, as well as in various parts of North and South America, in an unadulterated state, are natives of the Canary Islands, where they breed in pleasant valleys, and on the delightful banks of small rills, or streams. They were known in Europe as long ago as the beginning of the sixteenth century, as we are told, concerning their arrival, that, "A ship, which, in addition to other merchandize, had a multitude of Canaries on board, that were consigned to Leghorn, was wrecked on the coast of Italy, and the birds, thereby obtaining their liberty, flew to the nearest land." This happened to be Elba, where they found so propitious a climate, that they multiplied without the intervention of man, and probably would have naturalised themselves, had not the wish to possess them been so great as to occasion them to be hunted after until they were entirely extirpated. In Italy, therefore, we find the first tame Canaries, where they are still raised in great numbers. At first, their rearing in Europe was attended with considerable difficulty, partly because the mode of treating these delicate strangers was not sufficiently understood, but principally because males, chiefly, and not females, were introduced.

DESCRIPTION.

THE Canary bird is five inches in length, of which the tail comprises two inches and a quarter; the beak is five lines long, stout, sharply pointed, and whitish; the legs are flesh-

CANARIES AND NEST.

colored, and eight lines high. The female is scarcely to be distinguished from the male, but the latter has generally deeper and brighter colors; the head is rather thicker; the body, in general, more slender throughout; and the temples and the space around the eyes, are always of a brighter yellow than the rest of the body.

The original grey color of this bird, which merges into green beneath, has, by means of domestication, climate, and inter-mixture with other birds, become so multifarious, that Canaries may now be met with of almost every hue; but grey, yellow, white, blackish and reddish-brown, are the prevailing colors, which are individually seen in every degree of shade, or com-bination, and thus present innumerable differences. Those which are of a blackish-grey, or greyish-brown, above, with greenish-yellow beneath, like a greenfinch, are the most com-mon, generally the strongest, and approach the most closely to the original color of their primogenitors. The yellow and white ones have usually red eyes, but are more delicate. The chestnut-colored are the most rare, and in strength and length of life are intermediate. The colors of most Canaries consist of a mixture of these, and that bird is the most prized the more regularly it exhibits the combination of these various shades. That which is most generally admired, at present, is one with yellow, or white, upon the body, and of a dun-yellow color on the wings, head, and tail. Next in degree of beauty, is that which is of a golden yellow, with a black, blue, or blackish-grey head, and similar wings and tail. There are also blackish or grey ones, with yellow heads, or with a ring about the neck, white, with brown and black markings, ashy-grey, almost black, with a yellow breast, and white head and tail, all of which have a prominent value. Others, which are irregularly marked, and are variegated, or mottled, are less esteemed.

HYBRIDITY.

As remarked in a preceding page, the original color of the Canary bird is grey, which merges into green beneath, almost resembling the colors of the linnet; but by means of domes-tication, climate, and intermixture with other birds, as the citril finch and serin, of Italy, and with the Siskin and linnet,

of Germany, they have become so multifarious, that they are
to be met with of almost every color and hue. Furthermore,
in Europe, there are societies for promoting the breeds, and
premiums are awarded to competitors who come nearest to the
model of perfection given out for competition. The hybrids
produced by crossing the Canary with other birds, most in
favor, may be described as follows:—

1. *The Cross between the Canary and Goldfinch.*—The colors
of this variety consist of a very beautiful intermixture of those
of both parents. One which has been highly prized, was
marked in the middle of the crest with ashy-grey; the rest of
the head, and the upper part of the neck, was of a silvery
white, with a bright orange-red ring round the base of the
beak, and another ring of snowy whiteness round the neck;
the back was greyish-brown, striped with black; the rump,
white; the under part of the body, snow-white; the vent, the
wings, and the first pinion feathers, were also white; the rest,
as well as the coverts, black, edged with yellow, and with a
golden-yellow spot in the centre of the wings; the tail was
white, with a black lateral spot; the beak and feet, white, the
former with a black tip. The mother of this fine bird was
white, with a greenish crest. In general, the handsomest
varieties are produced when yellow or white Canaries are
pared with goldfinches.

2. *The Cross between the Canary and the Siskin.*—This is per-
fectly like the female Siskin, if the male bird is a green
Canary, but if the latter be white or yellow, it becomes
rather brighter and always retains the color and figure of the
Siskin.

3. *The Cross between the Canary and the Serin* is distinguished
only by its smaller size, and by its short, thick, beak, from the
common grey or green Canary, unless produced by a white or
yellow hen.

The Cross between the Canary and the Linnet.—When the
offspring of a grey Canary, its only difference is a slightly
longer tail; but it is variegated or speckled when the Canary
is yellow or white.

PAIRING AND LAYING.

In order to obtain birds of a brilliant plumage, it is requisite to pair together such as are of similar markings, and the colors of which are regular and distinct. This is best effected in separate breeding cages. Variegated and checkered ones are often produced in aviaries where the birds pair together indiscriminately. Those of a greenish and brownish color, paired with bright-yellow ones, often produce beautiful dusky-white, or other favorite colors. A requisite precaution to be observed is, that a tufted and a smooth-headed bird should be paired together; for, if two crested ones be placed with one another, a part of the head of their progeny will be bald, or otherwise deformed.

Some males are always dejected, sing but little, are indifferent to their mates, and consequently unfit for breeding; others are too choleric, incessantly snap at, and chase about, the females, and indeed, often kill them and their young; others, again, are too ardent, persecute the female while she is sitting, tear the nest, throw out the eggs, or continually excite her to pair, until she quits her eggs or neglects her young; others, in breeding time, sing so incessantly, and so powerfully, that they rupture the small vessels of the lungs, and suddenly drop dead in the midst of their song.

The females have also their defects. Some merely lay, and immediately quit their eggs as soon as laid; others feed their young badly, bite them, or pluck out their feathers; others lay with much exertion and labor, and when they should hatch become sickly, or lay again after a long interval.

Those birds which are to be paired for the first time, should be placed together in a small cage or an open room for a week or ten days, to be wonted to one another. If two females are to be paired with one male, they must previously be accustomed to each other's society by being also kept together in a small cage; and the breeding cage should have two compartments, separated by a board, in which a sliding door has been made. In one compartment, a lively male may be enclosed with a female. About the cage or room, there should be placed some flax, soft hay, wool, hog's bristles, cow's hair, moss, pieces of thread, cut about a finger's length, paper, shavings, or other dry materials for building the nest, which usually occupies three days. When one female has laid eggs, the sliding door may be moved and the male admitted to the other female; and when they have both laid, this door may be

CANARY BREEDING CAGE.

kept open. The male will visit both females alternately, when they will not trouble themselves about each other; otherwise, without this precaution, jealousy would incite them to destroy each other's nests and throw out the eggs. In a room or aviary, a male has sometimes two and even three females placed with him; with one of these, he will more especially pair. But when this favorite is about to sit, the others will receive a share of his attentions, and from the latter usually the greatest number and the best birds are reared.

The female, as with the majority of birds, is usually the architect, the male only selecting the place and procuring materials, the coarser of which is used for the external structure, and the finer for lining the inside of the nest. The females will sometimes show indications of their instinct by building nests after their own fashion, generally being irregular in figure, and not nicely finished, at least externally. It is in the nest itself, where the pairing takes place, the female attracting the male by a continuous piping note, repeated more quickly the nearer she is to laying. An interval of seven or eight days elapses between the first pairing and laying the first egg. Every day afterwards, nearly at the same hour, an egg is laid, the number varying from two to six.

BREEDING, INCUBATION, ETC.

The month of March is the best time to place the birds in the breeding cage. Of these, there are two kinds, either a large one, made of wire, as is shown at page 15, in which it is better to place a male, and one female, than one male and two females together, like the one shown in the preceding page; or the birds may have range of an entire room. All breeding places must be exposed to the warmth and light of the sun, and be hung about with nests made of turned wood, tin, or little wicker baskets, two for each pair.

When a room is allotted to the purpose, it ought to contain shrubs for the birds to perch or build upon, with a plenty of fresh water to drink and bathe in, that being indispensable for all birds. The light should be admitted into the east or south-east, for the benefit of the morning sun, and the windows should have wire cloth over them, that the birds may enjoy the fresh air. The floor of the apartment should be strewed with clean gravel or sand, on which should be thrown celery or chickweed; but when breeding, they should have nothing except hard-chopped eggs, dried roll, cake without salt, and once in two or three days a few poppy seeds.

When the birds are good breeders, it is needless to attempt to assist nature by artificial means; and it is best to leave the them entirely to themselves. In other cases, it is customary to remove the first egg and replace it by an ivory one, placing it in a box filled with clean, dry sand, and so taking away all the eggs till the last one is laid; all are then returned to the nest to be hatched. They often lay three or four times a-year, from February to September, and some are so assiduous in pairing, that even moulting does not interrupt them. The eggs are of a sea-green color, marked on one end with reddish-brown or violet spots or stripes. The period of incubation lasts thirteen days.

If, from the sickliness of the male, or of the female, any of the eggs are unimpregnated, they must be taken out of the nest when the hen has sat for a week or ten days, held lightly between the fingers in the sunshine, or in a bright light; the fecundated ones will then appear filled with veins, while the bad ones will be quite clear, or already addled, the latter of which must be thrown away. The male rarely relieves the female in hatching, nor does she very willingly permit it. Immediately after feeding, she returns to the eggs, and should the male perchance be on the nest at the time, if he should not directly quit, he would speedily be compelled to do so by pecks and blows. The young are occasionally killed in the egg, in consequence of loud and near noises, such as heavy thunder, the discharge of fire arms, violently slamming the door, or any other very loud knocking.

FEEDING AND REARING THE YOUNG.

As soon as the young are hatched, the old birds should be supplied with one fourth of a hard-boiled egg, minced very fine, with some dried roll, or bread, containing no salt, steeped in water, the latter of which should be squeezed or pressed out again. In another vessel, some boiled rape seed should be placed, which has been rewashed in fresh water, to take away the acidity. Some use crackers instead of bread, but this is unnecessary. It is merely requisite to see that this soft food does not become sour, otherwise it will kill the young, and the cause remain unsuspected. Some persons merely give them their usual food, intermixing it with some finely-powdered crackers and hard-boiled eggs, but it has been found by experience, that the diet prescribed above is more efficacious, especially until the young are fledged.

It is now that the male takes the chief part in rearing the young; and upon him devolves the duty of feeding them, in order to allow the female to recover from the exhaustion she has received from incubation.

If it is necessary to feed the young by hand, grated roll or pulverised dry crackers is taken, mixed with pounded rape seed, and kept in a box. As often as it is necessary to feed them, a little of it is moistened with some of the yolk of an egg and water, and given to them from a quill pen. This must be done ten or twelve times a-day; about four penfuls is the quantity necessary for each meal.

Up to the twelfth day, the young remain almost naked, and require to be covered by the female; but after the thirteenth, they will feed themselves. In cold, dry years, however, it sometimes happens that the birds get scarcely any plumage at all. When they are a month old, they may be removed from the breeding cage. With the usual food of the old birds, they must be fed for some time upon the kinds above named; for, the sudden removal from soft food often occasions death, especially in moulting. It is asserted, and not without reason, that those Canaries which are reared in an arbor, where they have space to fly about within an enclosure of wire, are longer-lived and stronger than those which are reared in a chamber or a confined cage.

It is a curious fact, perhaps not known to every one, that, when there are two females with one male in a cage, and one dies, the other, if she has not already sat, will hatch the eggs laid by her co-mate, and rear the young as her own; and, during this foster-mother care, cautiously avoid the caresses of the male!

TO TEACH A YOUNG CANARY TO SING.

WHEN the young birds can eat alone, say at the age of thirteen or fourteen days, and often before quitting the nest, the males commence warbling, and the females, also, but less connectedly and from this, the sexes may be distinguished. To teach a young Canary to sing, he must now be separated from his comrades, as well as from other birds, and placed in a small wire cage, which, at the commencement, must be covered with linen, and subsequently, by degrees, with thicker woollen cloth, when a short air, or other musical piece, must be whistled to him, or a flute, or a small organ may be used. This lesson should be repeated five or six times a-day, especially mornings and evenings, and in five or six months, he will be able to acquire the air, according to the power of his memory.

FOOD AND MANAGEMENT OF ADULT BIRDS

EXCEPT during the breeding season, the males may be kept in cages either bell-shaped or like that denoted in the adjoining cut. These may be made of wire or rattan, and should be at least a foot high and eight inches in diameter, with one or more transverse perches.

The female is allowed either to have freedom in the room with her wings clipped, or is placed in a large breeding cage, possessing sufficient space to keep her limbs in constant exercise, and preserve them in health and strength.

In the bell-shaped, or smaller cages, wherein it must be understood only one male should be put, both the eating and drinking vessels must be placed on the outside, at the extremities of the lower perch. These should be surrounded by a cap of tin, so that the bird may not easily scatter its food. Cleanliness will often prevent these delicate songsters from suffering many disorders, and it is very desirable that the

floor of the cage should be made movable, that it may be
more easily cleansed and strewed with coarse sand.

Being naturally inhabitants of a warm climate, and rendered delicate by constant residence in rooms, and so, in a
manner habituated to a temperature similar to that of their
own country, great care is necessary in winter, in order that
the same or a similar temperature may be preserved, avoiding
the exposure to cold air, which, however, refreshes in summer,

CANARY BIRD CAGE.

cannot be otherwise than prejudicial to them, causing sickness
and even death.   To keep these birds in a healthy and happy
frame, it is very important to observe that, in summer, they
be frequently hung in a cage in brilliant daylight, and if
possible, placed in the warm sunshine, which, especially wt-en
bathing, is very agreeable to them.

The most important consideration in the managemen of
the male is his food. The more simple and true to name

this is, the better does it agree with him; whereas, when too artificially compounded, it renders him sickly and weak. The best food is the "summer rape seed," which is sown in spring. This is distingnished from the "winter rape seed," which is sown in autumn, by being larger and of a darker hue. On this diet. these birds thrive very well, but it should be occasionally intermixed with some crushed hemp seed and Canary seed, for the sake of flavoring it; and this more especially in the spring, when they are intended for breeding. As a treat, we may occasionally give them a mixture of summer cabbage seed, whole oats or oatmeal, with millet, or some Canary seed. Here, as in most other cases, we should strive to imitate nature.

The hen Canaries may likewise be supplied with the same kind of food as the males; but in winter, they are content with bread, containing no salt, or merely barley grots, moistened in milk, if given to them fresh every day, without being sour. Besides, both males and females may be given, in summer, some green lettuce, cabbage, groundsel, and water cresses, which must be previously washed and cleansed from anything prejudicial; and in winter, they may be fed with pieces of sweet apples. They require fresh water daily, both for drinking and bathing; and at moulting time, a rusty nail should be occasionally placed in their drinking vessel, as this tends to strengthen the stomach.

TO TEACH THE ADULT BIRDS TO FLY.

CANARIES may be taught to fly; but the trouble and risk are so great that it is hardly worth the time and care necessary to teach them. The male is first allowed its liberty in a place where there are trees, and the female is hung at a window, near by, which speedily attracts him back to the cage in case of danger or fatigue. This teaching must be continued for five or six days, but no handling nor violent attempts to catch them should be used.

DISEASES.

THE Canary bird, in a state of captivity, seldom enjoying the open air and having but little exercise, is subject to most of the maladies peculiar to the domestic, feathered race. The diseases to which it is particularly liable, may be described and treated as follows:—

1. *Rupture.*—This is a common malady, especially in young birds, and is a kind of indigestion which causes inflammation of the intestines. The symptoms of this disease are a lean, transparent, blown-up body, full of small red veins, and in which all the intestines seem to have fallen to the lower part of the body, where they become entangled and turned black. Too much nutritious food is the cause of this evil. All remedies appear to have been ineffectual in this malady, but assistance is sometimes obtained from a spare and simple diet.

2. *The Yellow Gall in the Head and Eyes* may be cured by refreshing food; but if there be a tubercle of the size of a hemp seed about the head or eyes, it must be cut off, and the wound anointed with fresh butter.

3. *Sweating.*—Some females, whilst hatching, have a sweating sickness, which is injurious to the blood, and may be detected by the feathers of the lower part of the body being quite wet. The body of the bird should be washed with brine, and afterwards with rain or spring water to free the feathers of salt, and then rapidly dried by the sun or fire. This may be repeated once or twice a-day. This sickness, however, is not so prejudicial to the bird as is generally supposed.

4. *Sneezing.*—This is occasioned by a stoppage of the nostrils, and may be removed by a very small feather dipped in olive oil being passed through them.

5. *Loss of Voice.*—If the male, after moulting, lose his voice, he must have diet similar to that given to young birds; that is, some thoroughly-baked, stale roll, dipped in boiled milk or water until completely saturated; then press out the milk and

mix it with more or less, say a proportion of two thirds of coarse barley or wheat flour, freed from the husk or bran. Some persons give them a slice of pork or bacon to peck.

6. *Constipation* is cured by giving them plenty of green food, such as celery, water cresses, chickweed, sallad, &c.

7. *Epilepsy* is commonly brought on by too great a delicacy of treatment, and also by timidity, from alarm. Too great an abundance of rich food, and the want of proper exercise, whereby much and thick blood is produced, are the chief causes of this disease. The birds ought to be kept free from alarm, either by catching or tormenting them in any way. When suffering under this complaint, if they are hot, it is recommended to dip them frequently into cold ice water, and then pair their nails so closely as to start blood. A few drops of olive oil, also, given internally have proved serviceable.

8. *Overgrown Claws or Beaks* require to be pared with sharp scissors. Care must be taken, however, not to cut the nails too close, as the birds would be liable to lose so much blood as to become lame. The end of the "red ray," or vein, both in the beak and claws, when held up to the light, shows exactly how far they may be cut. During the hatching period, also, the nails of the female sometimes must be cut, in order that they may not be caught by them when in the nest.

9. *Lice* may be avoided by frequent bathing, cleanliness in the cage, and dry sand mixed with anise seed and scattered on the floor.

THE GOLDFINCH.

Synonymes.

Fringilla carduelis,	Of Ornithologists.
Chardonneret,	Of the French.
Distelfink, Stieglitz,	Of the Germans.
Jilguero,	Of the Spaniards.
Pintaçilgo,	Of the Portuguese.
Calderino,	Of the Italians.
Goldfinch, Thistle Finch,	{ Of the British and Anglo-Americans.

OF all cage birds, this is one of the most delightful, alike from the beauty of its plumage and the excellence of its song, its proved docility, and remarkable animation, whose body is almost always in incessant motion—now moving to the right and now to the left. Its song is shrill, agreeable, and heard during all seasons, excepting only at the period of moulting. It contains, besides many warbling and twittering notes, on which it dwells more or less, and the oftener the syllable *fink* is repeated the more it is admired. Some utter these notes only once or twice in their song, and others four or five times in succession. They also repeat airs, and the songs of other birds, but with difficulty; for they have not the same capacity as linnets and Canaries for these acquisitions.

Their docility is extraordinary, for they will even learn to fire small cannons and imitate death. They may also be taught to draw up their food and water in a little bucket.

Mr. Syme, in his excellent treatise on British Song Birds, gives the following amusing particulars respecting this species:—"The goldfinch is easily tamed and easily taught, and its capability of learning the notes of other birds is well known; but the tricks it may be taught to perform are truly astonishing. A few years ago, the Sieur Roman exhibited his birds, which were goldfinches, linnets, and Canaries. One appeared dead, and was held up by the tail or claws without exhibiting any signs of life; a second stood on its head with its claws in the air; a third imitated a Dutch milkmaid going to market with pails on its shoulders; a fourth mimicked a Venetian girl looking out at a window; a fifth appeared as a soldier, and mounted guard as a sentinel; and the sixth acted as cannoneer, with a cap on its head, a firelock on its shoulder, and a match in its claws, and discharged a small cannon. The same bird also acted as if it had been wounded. It was wheeled in a barrow, to convey it, as it were, to the hospital, after which it flew away before the company. The seventh turned a kind of windmill; and the last bird stood in the midst of some fireworks, which were discharged all round it, and this without exhibiting the least symptom of fear."

The Goldfinch is very generally distributed throughout Europe, occurring in most of the wooded and cultivated districts. Its song commences about the end of March, and continues till July or August. It may often be found in company with linnets, whose flight it somewhat resembles.

DESCRIPTION

THE goldfinch is five inches and three quarters long, of which the tail occupies two inches. The beak is five lines long, sharply pointed, and very slightly bent, compressed at the sides, whitish, with a horn-colored tip; the slender feet are brownish, and six lines high; the front of the head is of a bright scarlet red; a broad margin of a similar color surrounds

the base of the beak; the chin and reins, black; the vertex
black, terminating in a stripe, which passes the back of the
head, and descends the neck on each side; on the top of the
neck, there is a white spot; the cheeks and front of the neck,
white; the back of the neck and back are of a beautiful
brown; the rump whitish, with a brownish tinge; the longer
feathers are black; both sides of the breast and the flanks of a
bright-brown; the middle of the breast, the belly, and the
vent, whitish, many of the feathers having a brownish tinge;
the thighs, greyish; the pinion feathers, velvet-black, with
whitish tips, which are smallest in old birds, and are sometimes
wanting in the first two feathers; the middle of the external

THE GOLDFINCH.

web with a golden-colored stripe an inch long, which, in con-
junction with the golden yellow tips of the hinder large coverts,
forms a beautiful spot; the coverts otherwise black; the tail
slightly forked and black; the two, and sometimes the first
three pinion feathers having a white spot in the centre of the
inner web; the rest with white tips, sometimes also the third
is likewise entirely black at the sides.

The female is a little smaller, not so broadly and beautifully
red about the beak; the chin brownish; the cheeks intermixed
with bright-brown; the small coverts of the wings, brown, and
the back of a deeper dark-brown.

BREEDING.

THE female goldfinch rarely lays more than once a-year,
(consequently these birds do not greatly multiply,) and then

from four to six eggs, which upon a pale sea-green ground are
marked with pale-red spots and dots, and deep-red stripes. The
young are fed from the crop. These, before they first moult,
are grey upon the head. They can be reared upon poppy
seeds and roll steeped in milk or water. They have greater
facility in imitating the song of the Canary than that of any
other bird; and with this bird they will produce fertile hybrids.
To effect this, a male goldfinch is placed with one or two hen
Canaries, and they very readily pair, especially if the goldfinch
has been reared from the nest. The birds which spring from
this union are not only beautiful in color and plumage—often
yellow, with the head, wings, and tail of the goldfinch—but
they will be found to excel in the sweetness and variety of
their song. If you are apprehensive that a pair of valuable
Canaries will not thoroughly hatch their eggs, nor let their
young ones die, remove them to the nest of a goldfinch; they
will not only hatch them, but will also feed the young, which,
when nearly full fledged, may be placed in a cage until they
can feed themselves, when no further trouble attends their
rearing.

The characteristics which mark the principal varieties of
this species are as follows:—

1. *Goldfinch* with a yellow breast.
2. *The White-headed Goldfinch.*
3. *The Black-headed Goldfinch.*
4. *The White Goldfinch.*
5. *The Black Goldfinch.*

The latter are either entirely black, which is caused by
age or in being fed upon hemp seed, or they retain the yellow
spots on the wings. Mr. Shelbach, of Cassel, in Germany,
reared a nest of goldfinches, which he kept entirely secluded
from the light of the sun, covering the cage with cloth.
These birds were of a jet-black, with yellow spots, but
they changed color after moulting. Those goldfinches which
become black before old age, usually resume their former
color after moulting, but then they do not usually live much
longer.

FOOD.

The goldfinch feeds upon various kinds of seeds, groundsel, succory, salad, cabbage, rape, linseed, Canary, thistle, and alder seeds, &c. In the cage, it must be fed upon poppy seed and hemp seed, the first being given as its usual food. If allowed to run freely about, it will accustom itself to the second description of universal food described at page 13. It may also have given to it all sorts of green things, such as salad, cabbage, lettuce, and water cresses. It eats voraciously, and therefore, when allowed to run about in the chamber, perches upon the trough, and chases away, with a threatening gesture, every bird that approaches; whereas, it will feed with other birds that have any kind of resemblance to it, at least with respect to the character of their food, such as Canary birds, Siskins, &c.

DISEASES.

These birds are very subject to epilepsy. If they happen to have bad and swollen eyes, they should be anointed with fresh butter. Heaviness and greediness, occasioned by feeding too exclusively upon hemp seed, may be removed by giving them in lieu of it soaked salad and thistle seeds. It contributes much to their health, if occasionally supplied with the head of a thistle.

In old age, they become blind, and lose the beautiful red and yellow colors of the head and wings. Although frequently subject to sickness, there are instances of their having lived to the age of sixteen and even twenty-four years.

THE LINNET.

HE linnet, from its natural flute-like voice, excels most other song birds in its power of beautifully and purely imitating melodies and airs which are piped to it, and for this quality it is especially esteemed. It will also learn the song of all the birds in the room or cage that it hears. Its natural song consists of many connected strophies, and is the more beautiful the oftener it utters some high-sounding notes, which are called its "crowing," from its resemblance to the crowing of a cock. It sings both summer and winter, excepting the time of moulting.

DESCRIPTION.

THE length of this bird is more than five inches, of which the tail measures two inches and a half. The beak, six lines long, is dusky-blue in summer, and in winter greyish-white, with the

point brown; the iris dark-brown; the feet, eight lines high,
are black. There are some very striking varieties produced
by the season and age in the plumage of the male, which are
not observed in the female, and these have caused great confusion in works on birds.

A male three years old or less, is distinguished in spring by
the following colors, and by the name of "red pole:"—The
forehead is blood-red, the rest of the head reddish ash-colored,
the top rather spotted with black; the cheek, sides of the neck,
and the circle round the eyes, have a reddish-white tint; the
feathers of the back are chestnut, with the edges lighter; the
upper tail coverts are black, edged with reddish-white; the
throat and under part of the neck are yellowish-white, with
some dashes of reddish-grey; the sides of the breast are

THE LINNET

blood-red, edged with reddish-white; the sides of the belly are
pale rust-colored; the rest of the under part of the body is
reddish-white; the greater wing coverts are black, bordered
with reddish-white; the others are rusty-brown with a lighter
border. The quill feathers are black, tipped with white; the
first are edged with white nearly to the point; the narrow
beard forms a parallel white streak to the quill feathers; the
tail is black and forked; the four outer feathers on both sides
have a broad white border; that of the two middle feathers is
narrower, and reddish-white.

After moulting, in autumn, little red is seen on the forehead,
because the feathers become colored from the bottom to the top;
the breast has not yet acquired its red tint, for the white border
is still too wide; but when winter comes, its colors appear.

Males one year old have no red on the head, and more
dashes of black; the breast is pale-red, waved with pale and
dark; the under part of the feathers on the breast is only a
bright, reddish-grey brown; the edges of these feathers are of a
reddish-white; the back rust-color, having detached spots of
dark-brown and reddish-white. These birds are known under
the name of "grey linnets."

After the second moulting, if the reddish-grey feathers are
blown aside, blood-red specks may be discovered on the
forehead, and the red of the breast is only hidden by the
wide yellowish-white borders to the feathers; these are the
"yellow linnets," or the "rock linnets," as they are called in
Thuringia.

Besides these three different varieties of plumage of the
males, there are several clouded, produced by the seasons and
old age; for instance, the older they become, the redder the
head is. Birds brought up in the house never acquire the fine
red on the forehead and breast, but remain grey like the males
of one year old; on the other hand, old ones, red when brought
into the house, lose their beautiful colors at the first moulting,
and remaining grey like the young ones, are no more than
grey linnets.

This difference of color does not take place in the females,
which are smaller than the males; the upper part of the body
is grey, streaked with dusky-brown and yellowish-white, on
the rump, with greyish-brown and reddish-white; these spots
are more numerous on the breast; the wing coverts are a
dusky-chestnut. The females are distinguished in the nest by
the back being more grey than brown, and by the number of
streaks on the breast, which resemble that of the lark; bird
fanciers leave these in the nest and take only the males.

Linnets breed twice a-year, and lay each time from four to
six bluish-white eggs, covered all over with flesh-colored
and reddish-brown spots and stripes. The male birds may
be recognised in the earlier stage of their growth by the
white ring round the neck, and the white on the tail and
wings.

HYBRIDITY.

It is common for a male linnet to pair with a hen Canary, and hybrids produced by this means are easily reared, and can scarcely be distinguished from other grey Canaries, either from their appearance or song.

LINNET CAGE.

FOOD AND MANAGEMENT.

In confinement, linnets require nothing but summer cabbage seed,* which does not require to be soaked, as they are naturally seed-eating birds, having a powerful crop and stomach, and can therefore better digest it. Hemp seed, they must not have at all. They must not be too well fed in the cage; for, taking little exercise, they would soon die from over-feeding.

---

* Winter cabbage seed, which does not injure them at liberty, soon kills them in confinement.

They like salt, and, contrary to the general rule, it is therefore well occasionally to intermix some with their food; and this is an excellent preventive against various maladies. When linnets are allowed to run about, they readily feed with other birds on the universal paste. Some green food must occasionally be given them, as also sand and water, as they like to bathe and dust themselves.

It is best to keep them in square cages, as they are less subject to giddiness in these than in round ones, and sing better. They are not often allowed to range the room, as they are very indolent, remaining immovable in the same place, and running the risk of being trodden upon; but if a small tree or a roost be placed in a corner, they may be let out of the cage with safety, as they will remain perched there, only leaving it to eat or drink, and will sing all day long.

DISEASES.

The most common disorders of this species are constipation, atrophy, and epilepsy; but linnets in confinement will generally live from twelve to sixteen years.

THE AMERICAN GOLDFINCH.

Synonymes.

Fringilla tristis,	Of Ornithologists.
Chardonneret jaune,	Of the French.
Amerikanischer Distelfink,	Of the Germans.
Jilguero americano,	Of the Spaniards.
Pintaçilgo americano,	Of the Portuguese.
Calderino americano,	Of the Italians.
Yellow Bird, American } Goldfinch,	} Of the British and Anglo-Americans.

HIS very beautiful and familiar messenger of spring is known throughout this continent from the 49th parallel of north latitude to the savannas of Guiana and Surinam. As summer approaches, the males cast off their olive-colored winter suits, and appear in their temporary golden livery, with the front of the head, wings, and tail of a deep black, when they may be heard in concert, tuning their lively notes, several sitting on the same tree enjoying the exhilerating scene, basking and pluming themselves, and vying with each other in pouring forth their varied, soft, and cheerful song. When they sing all together, as they now do, it has a pleasing effect; their favorite note resembles the word *băbée,* or *măy bé,* the last syllable protracted and much higher than the first. They have also a note, which they utter when flying through the air, that sounds somewhat like the word *physician,* pronounced very rapidly. But the most beautiful part of their song, is, when they raise and sink their voices in such a delightful cadence, that their music, at times, seems " to float on the distant breeze, scarcely louder than the hum of bees;" it then breaks out, as it were, into a *crescendo*, which rends the air like the loud song of the Canary.

In confinement, the yellow bird soon becomes familiar and reconciled, its song being nearly as animated and sonorous as its transatlantic congener. According to Mr. Audubon, it is extremely hardy, often remaining the whole winter in the Middle States, and when deprived of liberty, will live to a great age in a room or cage. "I have known two instances," says he, "in which a bird of this species had been confined for upwards of ten years. They were procured in the market of New York, when in mature plumage, and had been caught in trap cages. One of them having undergone the severe training, more frequently inflicted in Europe than America, and known in France by the name of *galerien*, would draw water for its drink from a glass, it having a little chain attached to a narrow belt of soft leather fastened round its body, and another equally light chain fastened to a little bucket, kept by its weight in the water, until the little fellow raised it up with its bill, placed a foot upon it, and pulled again at the chain until it reached the desired fluid and drank, when, on letting go, the bucket immediately fell into the glass below. In the same manner, it was obliged to draw towards its bill a little charriot filled with seeds; and in this distressing, occupation was doomed to toil through a life of solitary grief, separated from its companions, wantoning on the wild flowers, and procuring their food in the manner in which nature had taught them."

The food of the American goldfinch consists chiefly of the seeds of the various species of thistles, lettuce, hemp, and sunflower; and in winter, when its more agreeable food is not found in sufficient abundance, it resorts to the fruit and seeds of the elder. It also collects the tender buds of trees, as well as the confervas of brooks and springs, as a variety of its usual fare.

These birds occasionally do some damage to gardens by their indiscriminate destruction of lettuce and flower seeds, and they are therefore often disliked by gardeners; but their usefulness, in other respects, far more than counterbalances the trifling injuries they produce.

After being caught in trap cages, they feed as if quite contented; but, should it happen to be in the spring that they lose their liberty, and have thus been deprived of the pleasures anticipated from the previous union of a mate, they linger for a few days, pine away, and die. They are very fond of washing and bathing themselves, in clear shallow water, when the weather is mild, after which, they are engaged in picking up particles of sand and gravel, from which the fancier may take a useful hint.

It is stated that it is more difficult to procure a mule, or hybrid, between this species and the Canary, than between the latter and the European goldfinch, although the cross has often been made with success.

THE AMERICAN ROBIN.

Synonymes.

Turdus migratorius,	Of Ornithologists.
Tourd emigrant, Grievo du Canada,	Of the French.
Auswanderer Drossel,	Of the Germans.
Tordo migratorio,	Of the Spaniards.
Tordo emigrante,	Of the Portuguese.
Tordo migrante,	Of the Italians.
American Robin, Robin Red-breast, Migrating Thrush, Red-breasted Thrush,	Of the British and Anglo-Americans.

THE American robin is a saucy familiar bird, fond of man's neighborhood, throughout North America, from the 56th parallel of north latitude to the table lands of Mexico, and is more frequently to be seen in our orchards and fields than in the denser woods. The confidence he reposes in us by taking up his abode in our vicinage; the frankness and innocence of his manners; the simplicity of his thrilling lays, delivered in all the artless energy of true love; and the peculiar pleasure with which we listen to his vocal powers, ever inspires us with attachment and universal respect. Besides, the endearing name he sometimes bears, recalls to mind the well-known legend, so oft repeated in our juvenile days, of the "favorite Robin Redbreast," said to have covered with a leafy shroud the lost and wandering "babes in the wood." He is commonly called "robin," though there is but little resemblance between him and his European congener, except in the single circumstance of his having a red breast.

EUROPEAN ROBIN.

The American robin, when reared in a cage, is of a lively and gentle disposition, docile, and seemingly content, and the melody and simplicity of his song, of which he is very lavish in confinement, renders him a special favorite. He sings well, readily learns to imitate lively parts of airs, and on the authority of Mr. Nuttall, some have been taught to pipe forth psalms even to so solemn a measure as that of "Old Hundred!" He also acquires a considerable capacity for mimickry, imitating the notes of many of the birds around him, as those of the pe-wee, blue bird, and whip-poor-will. At times, he becomes very tame, and will go in and out of the house with domestic confidence, appear uneasy when left alone, and will follow his owner, come to her call, peck at her finger, or kiss her mouth, with seeming pleasure. His principal song, both in confinement and at large, commences in the morning before sunrise, and at which time it is very loud, emphatic, and full.

The rufous color of the breast becomes deeper in those birds brought up in confinement, and the females are somewhat paler than the males. The young, during the first season, are spotted on the breast with dusk and white.

FOOD AND MANAGEMENT.

DURING the winter, according to Mr. Audubon, the robin feeds on the berries and fruits of our woods, gardens, and fields, and even of the ornamental trees of our cities and larger towns. The holly, sweet gum, gallberry, and the poke are those it first attacks; but as these fail, it feeds on the mountain ash, Carolinian cherry, and the azedarach. On the latter, in their annual migrations to Florida and the Southern States, these birds often glut themselves to such an inordinate degree, that they are sometimes found stupified by its narcotic power. In spring and summer, they devour worms and snails. They also pick up from the fields the seeds of maize.

In confinement, this bird feeds on bread soaked either in water or milk, and on most kinds of our native and edible fruits. Being equally fond of insects as when at liberty, he seizes on all that enter his cage, or come within his reach.

The robin is comparatively a hardy and long-lived bird, and instances are reported of its having been kept for nearly twenty years. It suffers much in moulting, even in a wild state, and when in captivity, it loses nearly all its feathers at once. In general, when due care is observed to cleanliness, it is freer from parasitic vermin than most other species.

THE SONG THRUSH.

Synonymes.

Turdus musicus,	OF ORNITHOLOGISTS.
Grive, Tourd,	OF THE FRENCH.
Singdrossel,	OF THE GERMANS.
Tordo cantador,	{ OF THE SPANIARDS AND PORTUGUESE.
Tordo,	OF THE ITALIANS.
Song Thrush,	{ OF THE BRITISH AND ANGLO-AMERICANS.

HE song thrush is one of the few birds whose clear and beautiful notes animates and makes pleasing the European woods. From the summits of the highest trees, it announces, by its varying song, resembling that of the nightingale, the approach of spring, and sings throughout the whole summer, especially in the morning dawn and evening twilight. For the sake of this song, it is kept by fanciers in a cage, whence evening and morning, even as early as February, it will delight a whole street by its loud and pleasing song, when hung outside of the window, or inside, so that the window be a little open. In Thuringia, it is reputed to articulate words. Its strophe was heard formerly more frequently than it is now. Only old and excellent birds still sing it. This thrush will live from six to eight years, if its food be varied.

3*

DESCRIPTION.

THIS species is eight inches and a half long, of which the tail occupies three inches and a half; the beak is nine lines long, horny-brown beneath, and from the middle to the base, yellow; the irides nut-brown; the feet pale lead-color, one inch high; the whole of the upper part of the body olive-brown; the throat whitish-yellow, with a black stripe extending down its sides; the sides of the neck and breast, pale reddish-yellow, with numerous dark-brown, heart-shaped spots: the abdomen white, with oval dark-brown spots; the inside coverts bright orange-yellow; the pinion feathers grey-brown; the tail feathers the same.

THE SONG THRUSH.

In the female, the two black lines of the throat consist of small stripes, and the breast is pale yellowish-white.

FOOD AND MANAGEMENT.

THE food of the song thrush, in a state of liberty, consists generally of earth worms, but in autumn they eat berries of all kinds. Earth worms constitute their chief sustenance, with which they also feed their young. They are easily fed in confinement, and the universal paste is an agreeable delicacy to them. Barley meal, or merely wheat bran, wetted with water is sufficient to nourish them. But to get them into a state fit for song, they must have a more generous diet, such as roll, bread, meat, and many other things which come to table, for they are not dainty. They are fond of bathing.

In confinement, this bird is usually placed within a trellis, or it is put into a large cage of any shape, but at least three feet and a half long, and nearly as high; for, being a large and wild bird, and in constant motion, it easily injures its plumage. It is best that such large birds should have a separate room appropriated to them, as their copious excrements smell offensively.

DISEASES.

THE most usual maladies to which this bird is subject are a stoppage of the feather glands, constipation, and atrophy.

THE MOCKING BIRD.

———

Synonymes.

Turdus polyglottus,	OF ORNITHOLOGISTS.
Polyglotte, Tourd poly- glotte, Grand Moqueur	OF THE FRENCH.
Vielzüngler Vogel,	OF THE GERMANS.
Tordo poligloto,	OF THE SPANIARDS.
Tordo polyglotto,	OF THE PORTUGUESE.
Tordo poliglotto,	OF THE ITALIANS.
Mocking Bird,	OF THE BRITISH AND ANGLO-AMERICANS.

THIS "unrivalled Orpheus of the forest and natural wonder of America," inhabits the whole continent from the state of Massachusetts along the Atlantic, including several of the West-India Islands, as far south as Brazil; and from the table lands of Mexico, along the very base of the Rocky Mountains to Oregon, and the western sources of the river Platte. In short, he appears to dwell permanently in the milder regions of the New World, in either hemisphere; and those bred north of the Delaware, on this side of the equator, are all that ever migrate, in autumn, to more congenial climes.

The mocking bird, though destitute of brilliant plumage, is delicate and symmetrical in his proportions and beautiful in his form. His motions are easy, rapid, and graceful, perpetually animated with a playful caprice, and a look that appears full of shrewdness and intelligence. He listens with silent attention to each passing sound, treasures up lessons

from anything vocal, and is capable of imitating with exactness, both in measure and accent, the notes of all the feathered
race. And, however wild and discordant the tones and calls
may be, he contrives with an Orphean talent, peculiarly his
own, to infuse into them that sweetness of expression, and
harmonious modulation which characterises this inimitable
and wonderful composer. With the dawn of morning, while
yet the sun lingers below the blushing horizon, our sublime
songster, in his native wilds, mounted on the topmost branch
of a tall tree or bush, pours out his admirable song, which,
amidst the multitude of notes from all the warbling host, still
rises pre-eminent, so that his solo is heard alone, and all the
rest of the musical choir appear employed as mere accom-
paniments to this grand actor in the sublime opera of nature.
Nor is his talent confined to imitation; his native notes are
also bold, full, and perpetually varied, consisting of short ex-
pressions of a few variable syllables, interspersed with imitations, and uttered with great emphasis and volubility, sometimes
for half an hour at a time, with undiminished ardor. These
native strains bear a considerable resemblance to those of the
brown thrush, with which he is so nearly related in form,
habits, and manners; but like him, rude from cultivated genius,
his notes are distinguished by the rapidity of their delivery, their
variety, sweetness, and energy. As if conscious of his unrivalled powers of song, and animated by the harmony of his
own voice, his music is, as it were, accompanied by chromatic
dancing and expressive gestures; he spreads and closes his
light, fanning wings, expands his silvered tail, and, with
buoyant gaiety and enthusiastic ecstacy, sweeps around, and
mounts and descends into the air from his lofty spray, as his
song swells to loudness, or, in sinking whispers, dies away.
While thus engaged, so varied is his talent, that it might be
supposed a trial of skill from all the assembled songsters of
the air; and so perfect are his imitations, that even the sportsman is at times deceived, and sent in quest of birds that have
no existence around. The feathered tribes themselves are
decoyed by the fancied call of their mates; or dive with fear

into the close thicket, at the well-feigned scream of the
hawk.

Soon reconciled to the usurping fancy of man, the mocking
bird often becomes familiar with his master; playfully attacks
him through the bars of his cage, or at large in a room; restless and capricious, he seems to try every expedient of a lively
imagination, that may conduce to his amusement. Nothing
escapes his discerning and intelligent eye nor faithful ear. He
whistles, perhaps, for the dog, who, deceived, runs to meet his
master; the cries of the chicken in distress bring out the
clucking mother to the protection of her brood. The barking
of the dog, the piteous wailing of the puppy, the mewing of the
cat, the action of a saw, or the creaking of a wheelbarrow
quickly follow with exactness. He repeats a tune of considerable length; imitates the warbling of the Canary, the lisping of
the indigo bird, and the mellow whistle of the cardinal, in a
manner so superior to the originals, that, mortified and
astonished, they withdraw from his presence, or listen in
silence, as he continues in triumph.

In the cage, also, nearly as in the woods, he is full of life and
action, while engaged in song; throwing himself round with
inspiring animation, and, as it were, moving in time to the
melody of his own accents. Even the hours of night, which
consign nearly all other birds to silence and rest, like the
nightingale, he oft employs in song, serenading the houseless
hunter and silent cottager to repose, as the rising moon
illumines the darkness of the shadowy scene. His capricious
fondness for contrast and perpetual variety appears to dete-
riorate his powers. His lofty imitations of the musical brown
thrush are perhaps interrupted by the crowing of the cock, or
the barking of the dog; the plaintive warblings of the blue
bird are then blended with the wild scream and chatter of the
swallow, or the cackling of the hen; amid the simple lay of
the native robin, we are surprised with the vociferations of the
whip-poor-will; while the notes of the garrulous jay, kildeer,
woodpecker, Baltimore wren, and many others succeed, with
such an appearance of reality, that we imagine ourselves

in the presence of the originals, and can scarcely realise the
fact, that the whole of this singular concert is the effort of a
single bird. Indeed, it is impossible to listen to these Orphean
strains, when delivered by a superior songster in his native
woods, without being deeply affected, and almost rivetted to
the spot, by the complicated feelings of wonder and delight, in
which, from the graceful and sympathetic action, as well as
enchanting voice of the performer, the eye is no less gratified
than the ear.*

DISTINCTION BETWEEN THE MALE AND FEMALE.

THE young male bird, which must be selected as a singer,
may be distinguished by the breadth and purity of the white
on the wings. This white spot, in a full-grown male, spreads
over the whole nine primaries, down to, and considerably
below, their coverts, which are also white, sometimes slightly
tipped with brown. The white of the primaries, also, extends to
the same distance on both vanes of the feathers. In the female,
the white is less clear, spreads only over seven or eight of the
primaries, does not descend so far, and extends considerably
further down on the *broad* than on the *narrow* side of the
feathers. The black is also more inclined to brown.

FOOD AND MANAGEMENT.

IN a state of freedom, the principal food of the mocking
bird consists of insects, grasshoppers, and worms. Dew-
berries from the fields, and many kinds of our cultivated
fruits, together with insects, supply the young as well as the
parents with food. In winter, they chiefly subsist on berries,
particularly those of the Virginia juniper, (red cedar,) wax
myrtle, holly, smilax, sumach, sour gum, and a variety of
others.

* Nuttall.

Successful attempts have been made to breed these birds in confinement by allowing them retirement and a sufficiency of room. Those which have been taken in trap cages are accounted the best singers, as they come from the school of nature, and are taught their own wild wood notes. The young are easily reared by hand from the nest, from which they ought to be removed at eight or ten days old. Their food is thickened meal and water, or meal and milk, mixed occasionally with tender fresh meat, minced fine. Animal food, almost alone, finely divided and soaked in milk, is at first the only nutriment suited for raising these tender nurslings. Young and old require berries of various kinds, from time to time, such as cherries, strawberries, whortleberries, &c., and, in short, any kind of wild fruits of which they are fond, if not given too freely, are useful. A few grasshoppers, beetles, or any insects conveniently to be had, as well as gravel, are also necessary; and spiders will often revive them when drooping or sick. But, notwithstanding all the care and management bestowed upon the improvement of this bird, it is painful to reflect that his extraordinary powers of nature, exercised with so much generous freedom in a state of confinement, are not calculated for long endurance; for, after this most wonderful and interesting prisoner has survived six or seven years, blindness often terminates his gay career—thus shut out from the cheering light of heaven, the solace of his lonely, though active existence, he now, after a time, droops in silent sadness and dies. At times, this bird is so infested with a minute species of louse as to be destroyed by it.

Good singing birds of this species generally command from $5 to $15 each, though individuals of extraordinary and peculiar powers have been sold as high as $50, or $100, each, and even $300 have been refused!

THE BROWN THRUSH.

Synonymes.

Turdus rufus,	OF ORNITHOLOGISTS.
Tourd roux,	OF THE FRENCH.
Rother Drossel,	OF THE GERMANS.
Tordo rojo,	OF THE SPANIARDS.
Tordo ruço,	OF THE PORTUGUESE.
Tordo rosso,	OF THE ITALIANS.
Brown Thrush, Ferruginous Thrush, Thrasher,	OF THE BRITISH AND ANGLO-AMERICANS.
French Mockirg Bird,	OF THE SOUTHERN STATES.
Red Mavy,	OF SOME PARTS OF NEW ENGLAND.

THIS large, cheerful, and familiar songster, inferior to none in musical talent, if we except the mocking bird, is found in almost every part of the United States from Canada to the shores of the Mexican Gulf, breeding, according to Mr. Nuttall, in all the intermediate space, though more abundantly towards the north. His voice somewhat resembles that of the European thrush, but is far more varied and powerful, rising pre-eminent amidst the forest choir. He takes no delight in mimicking the song of other birds, and therefore has no claim to the title of "mocking bird," as he is usually called at the south.

On the first appearance of this bird in the spring, he faulters in his song, like the nightingale, but when his mate commences the cares and labors incident to breeding and rearing her young, his varied and melodious notes are steadily poured out in all their vigor and strength. In the month of May, while the blooming orchards perfume the air and decorate the landscape, his enchanting voice, in his affectionate lay, seems to give grateful utterance for the bounty and teeming profusion of nature, and falls in pleasing unison with the harmony and beauty of the season. And even the young birds, in a state of solitary domesticity, without the aid of their parent's voice, already whisper forth in harmonious reverie the pathetic and sweet warble instinctive to the species.

Deprived of other society, in a state of captivity, the brown thrush is exceedingly familiar, cheerful, and capriciously playful. He courts the attention of his keeper, follows his steps, complains when neglected, flies to him when permitted to be at large, and gratefully sings and reposes when perched on his hand. In short, in all his actions, he appears capable of real and affectionate attachment; but, like many other animals, he is jealous of every rival, particularly any other bird, which he drives from his presence with unceasing hatred.

FOOD AND MANAGEMENT.

According to Audubon, the natural food of this species consists of insects, worms, berries, and fruits of all sorts, being particularly fond of ripe pears and figs. In winter, they resort to the berries of the sumach, holly, dogwood, and shrivelled wild grapes.

In a state of confinement, these birds may be reared in the same manner, and on the same kind of food as their congener, the mocking bird. In the autumn, of the first season, the young begin their musical studies, " repeating passages with as much zeal as ever did Paganini." By the following spring, their lessons are complete and the full powers of their song developed.

Like the American robin, the brown thrush suffers much in moulting, and often nearly loses all his feathers at once.

THE CAT BIRD.

Synonymes.

Turdus felivox,	Of Ornithologists.
Gobe-mouche brun de Virginie, Moucherolle de Virginie, Tourd miaulant,	Of the French.
Miauendrossel,	Of the Germans.
Tordo de maullido,	Of the Spaniards.
Tordo miante,	Of the Portuguese.
Tordo miagolare,	Of the Italians.
Cat Bird,	Of the British and Anglo-Americans.

NE of the most remarkable propensities of this quaint and familiar songster, which inhabits almost every part of North America from Mexico to Canada, and even Kamtschatka, is the unpleasant, loud, grating, and grimalkin-like mew, (*'pāy,*) that it often utters, on being offended or approached; and thus coupled with the name of a " wizzard animal," so much disliked by many, this delightful vocalist, which seeks out the very society of man, and reposes an unmerited confidence in his protection, is generally treated with undeserved obloquy and contempt.

" The cat bird," says Nuttall, " often tunes his cheerful song before the break of day, hopping from bush to bush, with great agility, after his insect prey, while yet scarcely distinguishable amidst the dusky shadows of the dawn. The notes of different individuals vary considerably, so that sometimes his song, in sweetness and compass, is scarcely at all inferior to

that of the ferruginous thrush. A quaintness, however, pre-
vails in all his efforts, and his song is frequently made up of
short and blended imitations of other birds, given however,
with great emphasis, melody, and variety of tone; and, like
the nightingale, invading the hours of repose, in the late
twilight of a summer's evening, when scarce another note is
heard but the hum of the drowsy beetle, his music attains its
full effect, and often rises and falls with all the swell and
studied cadence of finished harmony. During the heat of
the day, or late in the morning, the variety of his song
declines, or he pursues his employment in silence and
retirement."

About the dawn of day, if at large, the cat bird flirts about with
affected wildness, repeatedly jerks his wings and tail, with a
noise somewhat resembling a whip, stretching forth his head,
opens his mouth, and mews. Sometimes this curious cry is so
guttural as to be uttered without opening his bill. He often
also gives a squeal as he flies from one place to another.

According to Latham, this bird is also capable of imitating
the variable airs of instrumental music, and will sometimes
mimick the cry of chickens so as to deceive and distress the
parent hen. When reared from the nest, he is easily domesticated, becomes a very amusing companion, and seems
attached to his cage. Although a pleasant songster, he is
seldom kept in confinement, and I believe all attempts at
breeding it, have failed.

FOOD AND MANAGEMENT.

THE natural food of this species is similar to that of the
ferruginous thrush, consisting principally of insects and
worms, particularly beetles and wasps, and the various kinds
of garden fruits.

In confinement, the food of these birds may be almost
everything that is vegetable, except unbruised seeds, such as
bread, fine pastry, containing little or no spices, cakes,

scalded Indian meal, juicy fruits, and now and then some bread boiled in milk, a few insects, or minced flesh. The young, when taken from the nest, may be fed on ripe cherries, and other kinds of juicy fruits.

"Like all other thrushes," says Mr. Audubon, "this is very fond of bathing and rolling itself in the dust or sand of the roads and fields. Several are frequently seen together in the borders o" small ponds or clear rivulets, immersed up to their body, splashing the water about them until completely wetted; then ascending to the top of the nearest bushes, they plume themselves with apparent care, notwithstanding which, they are at times so infested with a minute species of louse as to be destroyed by it."

THE EUROPEAN BLACKBIRD.

Synonymes.

Turdus merula,	OF ORNITHOLOGISTS.
Merle,	OF THE FRENCH.
Schwarzdrossel,	OF THE GERMANS.
Merlo,	OF THE SPANIARDS AND ITALIANS.
Melro,	OF THE PORTUGUESE.
Blackbird,	OF THE BRITISH.
English Blackbird,	OF THE ANGLO-AMERICANS.

BEING a permanent resident throughout the whole of the Old World, even as far north as Sweden, the European Blackbird is sufficiently hardy by nature to withstand the climate of nearly, if not all parts of the United States. Of all the thrushes, with perhaps the exception of the American robin, he is the most capable of instruction. His song is rich in melody, and contains some deep notes like those of the nightingale, varied, indeed, with some which are disagreeably harsh. At large, he sings only from March to July, especially at night; but in the cage, during the whole year except at moulting time. A single bird will enliven a whole street, so pure, distinct, and clear is his note. His memory, also, is so good, that he will learn several airs and melodies without mixing them; and sometimes even to imitate words. Neither does he forget what he has once well acquired.

DESCRIPTION.

THE European blackbird is about the size of the song thrush, nine inches and a half long, of which the tail comprises four inches. The beak is one inch long, and of a golden-yellow; the irides dark-brown; the feet black, and fourteen lines high. The male is entirely of a deep-black; the female black-brown, rusty-colored on the breast, and with an ash-colored tinge upon the abdomen; the throat, spotted with light and dark-brown; the beak and the feet, black-brown, appearing also to be rather larger and heavier, and hence it.has sometimes been considered a distinct species.

FOOD AND MANAGEMENT.

WHEN wild, the blackbird, like other species of thrush, feeds on all kinds of edible berries, such as the elder, cherry, and mountain ash; and when this food is not abundant, it satisfies itself with the tips of the white thorn. At this time, it often seeks for insects near the vicinity of warm springs.

In confinement, these birds are content with the first kind of universal paste, described at page 13, but will also eat bread, meat, and most kinds of food that comes to table. The young, which must be taken from the nest when their quills have but just sprung, can be reared upon roll steeped in milk.

The blackbird should be kept in a large cage, for it is not prudent to allow it to associate with other birds, as either through covetousness or caprice, it will attack the smaller kinds, and even peck them to death. Like all the allied species, this bird is fond of frequent bathing, and consequently should be amply supplied with the means. In captivity, he will live from twelve to fifteen years, especially if his food be varied.

DISEASES.

The blackbird is particularly subjec. to a stoppage of the oil gland, which may be softened by the application of fresh butter, mixed up with a good deal of sugar, the aperture being enlarged by gently distending it with a needle, or a small knife; but a lead salve, or rather a salve of litharge of silver, white lead, wax, and olive oil, which must be ordered at an apothecary's, opens it best. The usual remedy is to pierce it with a needle, or to cut off the hardened gland. If this evil have not yet too severely affected the health of the bird, it may be sought to be remedied by puncturing the gland, compressing it frequently, bathing the bird with a syringe, and plucking out some of the feathers of the tail. The accumulated fat is absorbed in the renewal of the feathers, when the gland resumes its natural functions.

THE RICE BUNTING.

Synonymes.

Icterus agripennis, Emberiza oryzivora,	OF ORNITHOLOGIS͟
Ortolan agripenne, Ortolan de riz,	OF THE FRENCH.
Reiss Ortolan, Fettammer von Carolina,	OF THE GERMANS.
Hortelano de arroz, Hortelano con plumas agrias,	OF THE SPANIARDS.
Cenchramo d'arroz, Cenchramo corn pennas agudas,	OF THE PORTUGUESE.
Ortolano di riso,	OF THE ITALIANS.
Rice Bunting, Rice Troopial, Rice Bird, Reed Bird, Boblink, Bob-o-link, Bob Lincoln, Bob Linkling, Skunk Blackbird, Meadow Bird, Butter Bird,	OF THE BRITISH AND ANGLO-AMERICANS.

HIS well-known and truly migratory bird, familiarly known to everybody by the name of "Bob Lincoln," who, as a stranger, perhaps, thinks it a point of politeness thus to announce himself, as he sits on a rail of the fence, or the branch of a tree, on his annual return in the spring from the south, inhabits the whole continent of America, from Labrador to Mexico; although his winter residence appears to be more confined to Cuba, Jamaica, and other West-India Islands than to the main.

In the month of May, these birds fix their abodes in the
"savannahs" of Ohio and Michigan, and the cool grassy
"meadows" of New York, Canada, and New England for the
purpose, principally, for hatching and rearing their young.
The song of the male continues, with but little interruption,
during the period of incubation, and his chant, at all times
very similar, is both singular and pleasant. "Often, like the
skylark, mounted and hovering on the wing, at a small height
above the field, as he passes along from one tree top or weed
to another, he utters such a jingling melody of short variable
notes, so confused, rapid, and continuous, that it appears
almost like the blending song of several different birds.
Many of these tones are very agreeable, but they are delivered
with such rapidity that the ear can scarcely separate them.
The general effect, however, like all the simple efforts of
nature, is good, and when several are chanting forth in the
same meadow, the concert is very cheerful, though monotonous,
and somewhat quaint. Among the few phrases that can be distinguished, the liquid sound of *Bob-ŏ-lee*, or *Bob-o-link*, *Bob-o-
linkè*, is very distinct.

"To give an idea of the variable extent of song, and even an
imitation, in some measure, of the chromatic period and air of
this familiar and rather favorite resident, the boys of this part
of New England, [Cambridge,] make him shout among others,
the following ludicrous dunning phrase, as he rises and hovers
on the wing near his mate:—' *'Bŏb-ŏ-link*, *'Bŏb-ŏ-link*, *'Tŏm
Denny*, *'Tŏm Denny*—' Come *pay me* the *twŏ-ănd-six-pence* you've
*owed more than a year ănd ă half ego!—'tshĕ 'tshĕ 'tshĕ, 'tsh 'tsh
'tshĕ,'* modestly diving at the same instant down into the grass,
as if to avoid altercation. However puerile this odd phrase
may appear, it is quite amusing to find how near it approaches
to the time, and expression of the notes, when pronounced in a
hurried manner."*

This relish for song and merriment, confined wholly to the
male, diminishes as the period of incubation advances, and
when the young brood begin to flutter around their parents,

* Nuttall.

the song becomes less frequent. Sometimes the female is inclined to have a second brood, for which preparation is made while she is yet engaged in rearing the first; but the male generally loses his musical talent about the first week in July; from which time, or perhaps earlier, his spring or pied dress begins gradually to be laid aside for the more humble brownish-black and brownish-yellow garb of the female, the whole, both old and young, then appearing nearly in the same songless livery, uttering only a *chink* of alarm when surprised.

When the voice of the male begins to fail, with the progress of the exhausting moult, he flits over the fields in a restless manner, and merely utters a broken *'bŏb'lee 'bŏb'lee*, or with his songless mate, at length, a *'weet 'weet, b'leet b'leet*, or a noisy and disagreeable cackling chirp. But at the early dawn of day, while the tuneful talent of the species is yet unabated, the effect of their awakening and faultering voices, jingling throughout the wide expanse of meadows is singular and grand. These sounds mingle like the noise of a distant torrent which alternately subsides and rises on the breeze, as the performers awake or relapse into rest; finally, they become more distinct and tumultuous, till, with the opening day, they assume the intelligible character of their ordinary song.

From the varied and changing plumage of this pleasing, and in some respects ludicrous bird, as well as for the singularity of his song, he is eagerly sought after by fanciers, and usually commands a fair price. Large numbers are annually captured in the Northen States in trap cages and fed, almost immediately after which, they resume their song. Many are purchased and carried to Europe, often to the disappointment of the adventurer, in regard to his profits, as, by the time they reach their destination, they change their livery and cease to sing.

FOOD AND MANAGEMENT.

The food of the rice buntings varies according to the season and locality in which they reside. Although on their early arrival at the north it consists of grubs, worms, caterpillars, beetles, grasshoppers, crickets, ground spiders, &c., they frequently feed on the seeds of dandelions and docks, the former of which are oily and sweet. Later in the season, and previous to leaving their native regions, they feed principally on various kinds of grass seeds, paricularly those of millet or other allied species (Panicums). If short of other food, they also attack the ripened fields of barley, wheat, and oats, in which they show their taste for plunder, and flock together like other blackbirds.

About the middle of August, vast parties of these birds enter the states of New York and Pennsylvania on their way south, where, along the margins of the large rivers, they find an abundant means of subsistence, during their short stay, on the seeds of wild rice (Zizania). As soon as the cool nights of October set in, and the wild rice crops begin to fail, these birds take their departure from New Jersey and Pennsylvania, and in their further progress through the Southern States, they congregate in large numbers in the rice fields, upon which they greedily feed, and, before the crop is gathered, they have already made their appearance in Cuba and Jamaica, where they subsist on the seeds of the Guinea grass, (Sorghum,) and become so fat as truly to deserve the name of " butter birds," and are highly esteemed for the table.

In a state of captivity, the food of this bird, during spring and summer, should resemble as nearly as possible that of nature; but in winter, he may be fed on rice, boiled in milk, millet, Canary seeds, wheaten bread, soaked in water, and minced animal food, containing no seasoning nor salt.

THE RAVEN.

Synonymes.

Corvus corax,	Of Ornithologists.
Corbeau,	Of the French.
Gemein Rabe, Kolkrabe,	Of the Germans.
Cuervo,	Of the Spaniards.
Corvo,	{ Of the Italians and Portuguese.
Raven, Crow, Corby,	{ Of the British and Anglo-Americans.

F all birds which have a convex, round, knife-shaped bill, furnished at the base with hair projecting forwards, in other words, of all that belong to the tribe of crows, this, from the breadth of its tongue, is the most easily taught to imitate the human voice. On the ground, he walks in a stately manner, his motions exhibiting a kind of thoughtful consideration almost amounting to gravity. His ordinary voice consists of a hoarse croak, resembling the syllable *cröck* or *crück*; but he frequently emits a note not unlike the sound of a sudden gulp, or the syllable *clück*, which he seems to utter when in a sportive mood; for, although ordinarily grave, the raven sometimes indulges in a frolic, performing somersets and various evolutions in the air. When divination formed a portion of the popular belief in Europe, this bird was held in considerable repute. Trouble was even taken to study its actions and all the circumstances attending its flight, and the various modulations of its voice. Of these, sixty-four different variations were enumerated, without including the more delicate intonations, exceedingly difficult to distinguish, to detect which, however, an excessively fine ear was requisite, as its cry, *crŏck* and *crŭck*, is so simple! Every distinct change had its peculiar signification, and there were not wanting people

THE RAVEN.

who studied to acquire this knowledge, while others carried their folly so far as to believe that, by eating the heart and viscera of this bird, they could acquire its prophetic powers.

The raven may be said to possess a social disposition; for, after the breeding season has passed, flocks are often seen in the northern parts of Europe and the adjacent islands, amounting to one or more hundreds. These birds can perceive an object, as a dead carcass, at a great distance, but that they can smell carrion a quarter of a mile off, we have no satisfactory proof, neither need we believe that they can; for as we may account for the phenomenon by their sight, it is unnecessary to have recourse to their other faculties. Ravens have character in their flight, as men have in their walk. A poet sauntering by a river, a conchologist or fisherman hunting along the shore for shells, a sportsman searching the woods and fields for game, a lady running home from a shower, or a gentleman retreating from a mad bull, move each in a different manner, suiting the action to the occasion. In like manner, ravens, as well as other birds, might communicate intelligence, perhaps, several miles distant, judging by the flight of their neighbors, that they had a prize in view. In this way, a system of telegraphing could be extended over a large extent of country, and a great number of birds might be made to assemble in a single day.

When domesticated and treated with kindness, the European raven, as well as our native variety, becomes attached to his owner, and will follow him about the garden or house, with all the familiarity of a confiding friend.

FOOD AND MANAGEMENT.

ALTHOUGH the raven is omnivorous, its chief food is carrion, by which is here meant the carcases of sheep, horses, cattle, deer, and other quadrupeds, dolphins and cetaceous animals in general, as well as fishes that have been cast ashore. In autumn, it sometimes commits great havoc among grain, and in spring, it occasionally destroys young lambs. It has also been accused of killing diseased sheep by picking out their eyes; but of this there is no satisfactory evidence. It annoys the housewives sometimes by flying off with young poultry, and especially by breaking and sucking eggs which the ducks or hens may have deposited, as they frequently do, among the herbage.

When these birds are intended to fly about, the young must be removed when half fledged, about twelve days after they are hatched, and fed upon meat, snails, and earth worms; they are also accustomed to eat bread and roll steeped in milk. The description of food they seek, when at large, as young hares, birds, eggs, mice, young geese, chickens, snails, pears, cherries, &c., renders them partly injurious and partly beneficial.

This bird can be allowed to run at large, or fly about, and if reared from the nest, which must be the case if he is to be taught to speak, he will return to the place of feeding, upon calling him *Jäck*, the name he usually bears. All glittering metal, especially gold, must be hidden from him, or he, like some other bipeds, will carry it off. To facilitate his speaking, or to give his tongue greater freedom, which is necessary for articulate sounds, the tongue chord is sometimes loosened with the view of increasing or heightening his powers of speech. Individuals, however, have been heard to speak with an unloosened tongue. The raven is naturally a long-lived bird, individuals having been known to live upwards of one hundred years.

PIGEONS.

THE ROCK PIGEON, OR WILD DOVE.

Synonymes.

Columba livia,	Of Ornithologists.
Colombe, Biset sauvage,	Of the French.
Holztaube,	Of the Germans.
Paloma toreaz, Paloma del campo,	Of the Spaniards.
Pombo bravo,	Of the Portuguese
Colombo salvatico,	Of the Italians.
Biset, Wild Rock Pigeon, White-Rumped Pigeon, Rock Dove, Wild Dove,	Of the British and Anglo-Americans.

THE rock or wild pigeon of Europe is well known as the inhabitant of the pigeon houses in various parts of the world, or "dove cots," as they are more frequently called, buildings expressly erected for the purpose of containing colonies of these birds. In this state, where they enjoy a perfect freedom of action, and are nearly dependant upon their

4*

own exertions for support, they can scarcely be called
"reclaimed," much less "domesticated." Man, indeed, has
only taken advantage of certain habits peculiar to the species,
and by the substitution of an artificial for a real cavern, (their
natural habitation,) to which the pigeon house may be compared, has brought it into a kind of voluntary subjection,
without violating, or at least greatly infringing upon its
natural condition, and has rendered it subservient to his
benefit and use.

DESCRIPTION.

In its natural state, the bill of this bird is blackish-brown;
the nostril membrane red, sprinkled, as it were, with a white
powder; the irides, pale reddish-orange; the head and throat,
bluish-grey; the sides of the neck and upper part of the
breast are dark lavender-purple, glossed with shades of green
and purplish-red; the lower part of the breast, abdomen, wing
coverts, as well as the upper mandible, bluish-grey, the greater
coverts and secondaries are barred with black, forming two

broad and distinct bars across the closed wings; the lower part of the back is white; the rump and tail coverts, bluish-grey; the tail, deep-grey, with a broad black bar at the end; the legs and feet are purplish-red; the wings, when closed, reach within half an inch of the end of the tail.

ORIGEN OF FANCY PIGEONS AND THE COMMON HOUSE DOVE.

It is from the wild rock pigeon, (*C. livia,*) that all those numerous varieties, or, as they are frequently termed, "races," of the common inhabitants of the dove cot have descended, which are so highly prized, and fostered with such care and attention by the fancier, or amateur breeder; for, however diversified their forms, colors, or peculiarity of habit may be, they are all considered as having originated from a few accidental varieties of the common house pigeon, and not from any cross of that bird with other species, no signs nor marks whatever of such being apparent in any variety known to us. In fact, the greater part of them owe their existence to the interference and art of man; for, by separating from the wild rock pigeon, such accidental varieties as have occasionally occurred, by subjecting them to captivity and *familiarisation,* and by assorting and pairing them together, as fancy or caprice suggested, he has, at intervals, generated all the various races, and peculiar casts, which, it is well known, when once produced, may be perpetuated for an indefinite period, by being kept separate from, and unmixed with, others; or, in other words, what is commonly termed breeding "in-and-in."

Indeed, the fact, that all the varieties, however much they may differ in color, size, or other particulars, if permitted, breed freely and indiscriminately with each other, and produce a progeny equally prolific, is another and a convincing proof of their common and self-same origin; for it is one of those universal laws of nature, which, if once set aside or not enforced, would plunge all animated matter into indescribable confusion, that the offspring produced by the intercourse of different, (that is, distinct species,) is incapable of further increase. That such an intercourse may be effected, is well known; but it is generally under peculiar or artificial circumstances, and rarely when the animals, birds, or whatever they may be, are in their natural state, and in a condition to make their own election. Thus it is in the crosses obtained in a state of confinement, between the Canary and goldfinch, linnet, &c. But in all these instances, the progeny are invariably "mules," and as a general rule, are incapable of further production; for although they may exhibit the passions natural to the sexes, and the females may produce eggs, which, in general, even with extreme care, are found addled and incapable of being hatched. Such, I may add, is the case with hybrids of some of the crosses themselves; for the mongrel progeny of the wild turtle dove, (*Turtur communis*,) of Europe, with the turtle of the aviary, (*T. risoria*,) has been proved, by frequent experiments, to be barren, although the two species whence it originated appear to be closely allied, and a mixed breed is easily procured; and such I am justified in saying, would be the event, if a cross could be obtained between the rock pigeon, (*Columba livia*,) and the European wood pigeon, (*C. œnas*,) or stock dove, as it is improperly called, or with the ring pigeon, (*C. palumbus*,) or any other species.

VARIETIES.

To describe or particularise all the varieties possessed by fanciers, would require a volume in itself; as, in addition to the permanent races, or those which, when kept pure, transmit their likeness to their offspring, there are intermediate casts produced by particular crosses between individuals belonging to the different varieties, and which, though highly prized in the first generation, are not considered worthy of further extension; as their progeny cannot be depended upon, but are found to degenerate, and are liable to run into still more distant and less-valued races.

Among the numerous varieties kept in aviaries by fanciers, which are deemed worthy of being perpetuated by breeding distinct, the following are held in particular esteem -

THE BROAD OR FAN-TAILED SHAKER.

This beautiful variety of the pigeon tribe receives the name of "fan-tail," from its habit of spreading out the feathers of its tail like a turkey cock, (for the same reason it is called *Pigeon paon* by the French,) and that of "broad-tailed shaker" from its breadth of tail, and a peculiar quivering motion of the neck, which is regarded as the attitude of courtship. From this motion, it is also sometimes called by the French *Pigeon trembleur paon*.

This bird has a full breast, and a short, handsomely-formed, arched neck, which it carries in a graceful swan-like curve. Its tail, according to the rules of the fancy, should consist, at the least, of twenty-four feathers; and at the most, of thirty-six, which number it should not exceed; for, if the tail be over-crowded with feathers, the bird suffers it to droop, a defect never overlooked, although the specimen may be faultless in every other respect.

Fan-tails, whose plumage is pure white, are more highly prized than those displaying red, yellow, blue, and black-pied colors; their carriage of the neck and tail being considered by far the most striking and elegant.

Some persons discriminate a variety which they call the
"narrow-tailed shaker;" but this is only a degenerate breed of
the fan-tail, or the result of a cross. Its neck is shorter and
thicker, back longer, and it has not so many tail feathers as the
broad-tailed shaker; neither does it expand its tail so fully, but
keeps the feathers rather closed one over the other, so as to
resemble a fan when some little way open. The color of its
plumage is generally white; but a few different tints, and even
an almond variety, are to be met with occasionally.

TUMBLERS.

These pretty pigeons are so called from their peculiar habit
of tumbling backwards in the air when on the wing; besides
which, they soar to so great a height as to be almost lost to the
view; when flying, they congregate very closely together; and
if they be good birds and accustomed to each other, they will
maintain such a compact flight, that a dozen may almost be
covered with a large handkerchief.

If the weather be warm and bright, they may be allowed to
wing their aerial gambols for four or five hours in succession;
but care must be taken, that no other species of pigeon mix
with them, for if they once become familiarised and fly with
others, they will gradually drop their highly-prized mode of
flight, and of course become worthless. They should never be
let out on a dull, heavy, misty morning, nor when a fog appears
to be rising, nor during a high wind; as all such atmospheric
variations, by causing desertions from their lofts tend to
diminish the stock. A hen tumbler should never be allowed
to fly while with egg.

The most esteemed tumblers do not somerset when swoop-
ing along, but only when they are beginning to rise, or when
coming down to pitch; and to preserve this, and the high-flying
properties in his stock, the provident fancier must spare no
expence in the purchase of one or two first-rate birds that have
been used to soaring, as they will be of much service in training the young ones.

When the birds are accustomed to their houses, they may be turned out upon the wing, but only once a-day. A bright grey morning is the best time, especially for young birds; and some hemp or Canary seeds must be scattered round their cots, to entice them in, when their hours of liberty have expired.

There is a particularly fine variety of this pigeon, which is called the "bald-pated tumbler," denoted by the cut below, from its having a beautiful snowy white head; it has pearl eyes, and in plumage is exceedingly diversified; the tail and flight feathers, however, match the head, which is pure white. When a tumbler, either of a black or blue color, has a long dash of white from the under jaw and cheek to a little way down the throat, it is called a "black" or "blue-bearded" bird,

BALD-PATED TUMBLER.

as the color may be; and if this beard be well shaped, and the bird be clean in the tail and flight, as before described, it may be reckoned very handsome and valuable. When these pigeons are dashing along in the brilliant sunshine, the lively contrast of their feathers adds much to the vivacity of their appearance.

There is another and still more beautiful variety of this breed, called by some fanciers the "ermine tumbler," but which is generally known by the name of the "almond tumbler." It is an extremely elegant, and highly-prized variety, and is derived from common tumblers judiciously matched; as yellows, duns, whites, black-splashed, black-frizzled, &c., so as to sort the feathers.

When in perfection, tumblers are esteemed by many persons to be the prettiest of all the pigeon tribe; and this high opinion is borne out by the beautiful diversity of their colors, which are so elegant and rich, in some birds, that they have been compared to a bed of tulips. The more they are variegated in the flight and tail, especially if the ground color be yellow, the more they are prized; and a fine bright-yellow ground has the precedence of all others, from its being so exceedingly difficult to acquire, that twenty light-colored birds may be procured for one displaying a deep, richly-tinted ground.

THE CARRIER.

The carrier, *Pigeon de Turquie*, of the French, is somewhat larger than most of the common pigeons; its feathers lie very close and smooth, and its neck is long and straight. From the lower part of the head to the middle of the upper chap, there is a lump of white, naked, fungous-looking flesh, which is denominated the "wattle;" this, in good birds, is met by two small swellings of similar flesh, which rise on each side of the under chap; and if this flesh be of blackish color, the bird is considered very valuable. The circle round the black pupil of the eye is usually of a brick-dust-red color; but if it be of a brilliant red tint, it adds considerably to the value of the bird; this circle is surrounded by another of naked fungous flesh, generally about the breadth of a half eagle, the greater the breadth of which, the more it is admired. When the incrusted flesh round the eye is very thick and broad, it shows that the pigeon will prove a good breeder, and will rear fine young ones.

The properties attributed to the carrier, and prized by fanciers, are three in the head, three in the eye, three in the wattle, and three in the beak. The properties of the head consist in its being flat, long, and straight; for instance, if the head be very long, narrow, and flat, it is reckoned, in shape, perfect; if the contrary, it is termed a "barrel head." The properties of the wattle of the eye are its breadth and circular, uniform shape; for, if one part appear to be more scanty than another, it is termed "pinch-eyed;" and is of comparative little value; while, if it be full, even, and free from irregularities, it forms a "rose eye," and is highly prized. The wattle should be wide across the beak, short from the head to the point of the beak, and lean a little forward from the head; as the bird is said to be "peg-wattled" if it lie flat. The beak must be black, long, straight, and thick; if it be an inch and a half in length, it is considered a long beak, but it must never measure less than an inch and a quarter; if the beak be crooked, (hook-beaked,) or spindle-beaked, the value of the bird is much diminished. This variety, in general, is either dun or black in color, although white, blue-splashed, and pied specimens occur; the black and dun birds are usually the most perfect in their properties; but as the blues, whites, and pieds are very rare, even inferior birds of these colors are of consider-value.

THE HORSEMAN.

Many fanciers suppose the "horseman" to be a cross breed, either between a tumbler and a carrier, or a pouter and a carrier, and then again bred from a carrier. In shape, it resembles the carrier, but it is smaller in all its proportions; its body being less, its neck shorter and the fungous-looking flesh round its eyes not exuberant, so that there is a greater space between the wattle on the beak, than that round the eye.

The most approved colors for this variety of pigeon are the blue, and blue-pied, as they are usually the best breeders. They should be flown twice a-day regularly, when young; and as they gain strength on the wing, they should be allowed to

THE HORSEMAN.

range loose, without any other birds in company. This variety is the kind generally employed in carrying letters; the genuine carriers being much too scarce and valuable to be commonly used.

THE POUTER.

All pigeons, as is well known, have the capability of inflating their crops with air; and a fine pigeon, with breast feathers glossed with metallic tints, strutting and bowing, with an inflated crop, around his mate, presents no uninteresting spectacle; but this remark will not apply to this bird. In the "English pouter," or "pouting horseman," there is nothing pleasing in its appearance nor graceful in its proportions; indeed, the inflation of the voluminous crop, rendering an erect, stiff, and apparently constrained attitude necessary, gives an aspect of distortion, or a want of a due balance of parts.

The pouter is of large size, often measuring eighteen inches in length from the tip of the beak to the end of the tail. The chest is not really voluminous, though it appears enormous when the crop is distended with air; the back is concave, and the tail ample; the tarsi are very long, and covered with downy feathers. These pigeons are of various colors, as blue, rufous, pied, or altogether white. Those birds which are tall, erect, with a very ample crop, and with the colors of the plumage regularly disposed, and according to certain fancy rules, are esteemed the most valuable.

The pouter is formed by a cross between the "dragon" and the "old Dutch cropper," which latter bird, except in the development of the crop, (whence its name,) had nothing to recommend it. From this intermixture, not without much care and expense, has resulted this favorite variety. The flight of the pouter is buoyant, but not rapid, nor capable of being long sustained. As varieties of the pouter, or rather as breeds allied to it, may be mentioned the "uploper" and the "Parisian pouter," said to be a beautifully-marked bird; but with these, I have no personal acquaintance.

Pouters are very expensive birds to rear, as the strain will soon become degenerate. As the old birds pay little attention to the wants of their young, it frequently happens that the tiny creatures are starved to death. Careful fanciers, therefore, never allow them to hatch their own eggs, but shift them as soon as they are deposited under a hen "dragoon," that has lately laid; and place the eggs of the latter bird under the pouter, in order that she may commence incubation; otherwise, she will lay again in a short time, which, often repeated, would, in all probability, kill her. Every pouter must be kept by itself during the winter season; and their coops must be lofty, so that they may not acquire a stooping habit, which is a very great fault. In the spring, every pair of pouters must have two pair of dragoons to tend and feed them; but care must be taken that the dragoons are kept in a loft separate from the pouters, as otherwise, a cross breed would probably be the result, and the stock become degenerate.

Pouting horsemen are not so much in repute as formerly, the "almond tumblers" having almost superseded them.

THE DRAGOON, OR DRAGON.

Dragons are bred between a tumbler and a horseman; and by frequently crossing them with the horseman, they acquire much strength and swiftness. They are exceedingly good breeders and kind nurses, and are, therefore, often kept as feeders for rearing young Leghorn "runts," pouters, &c.

The dragon is somewhat lighter and smaller than the horseman; and one of its chief beauties consists in the straightness of the top of its skull with that of its beak, which, according to the rules of the fancy, should form almost a horizontal line. These birds should be flown and trained while young, in the same way as the horsemen, which they are considered to surpass in swiftness, in short flights of from ten to twenty miles; but in longer distances, if the horsemen be well bred, they will far outstrip the dragoon.

THE JACOBIN.

This pigeon, often called a "Jack," is, when perfect in its properties, extremely rare. The real Jacobin is a very small bird, and the smaller it is, the more valuable; it has on the hinder part of its head, inclining towards the neck, a range of inverted feathers, in appearance like the cowl, or cap, of a monk; and from this peculiarity, it receives the sobriquet of " Jacobin," or " capper." These feathers are technically termed the " hood," and if they grow compact and close to the head, they enhance the value of the bird considerably; the lower part of the hood is called the " chain," and the feathers composing it should be long and thick.

THE JACOBIN.

A small head, very small spindle-shaped beak, and beautifully clean, pearl eyes are other properties of this little pet. Yellow, red, blue, and black are the colors usually bred, and in point of color, the yellow birds are preferred before all others; however, let the color of the body be what it may, according to the rules of the fancy, the tail, flight, and head must invariably be white; sometimes the legs and feet are covered with feathers.

THE CAPUCHIN.

In its properties, this variety is closely allied to the Jacobin, and is, by some fanciers, considered a cross between that breed and some other kind. It has a longer beak, and is altogether a larger bird, than the Jacobin; its hood is extremely pretty, but it lacks the chain.

THE MAWMET.

The Mahomet, commonly corrupted to " Mawmet," is a beautiful cream-colored bird, with bars of black across its wings;

although the surface of its feathers is of a cream-color, the part next the body, the flue feathers, and even the skin, are of a dark sooty tint; it is about the size of a "turbit," but it has in place of a frill, a fine gullet, with a seam of beautiful feathers; its head is thick and short, and its eyes orange-color, surrounded by a small, naked circle of black flesh; it has a little black wattle on its beak, which is short and stout, and somewhat resembles that of a bulfinch.

THE BARB.

This variety was originally brought from Barbary. In size, it is somewhat larger than the Jacobin; it has a short, thick beak, a small wattle, and a circle of thick, naked, incrusted flesh round its eyes; the wider this circle of flesh spreads round the eye, and the more brilliant its color, the more the bird is prized; the circle is narrow, at first, and is not fully developed until the bird is three or four years old.

The plumage of the Barb is usually dun or black; but there are pied birds of both colors; these last are held in little estimation, as they are supposed to be only half bred; when the pinion feathers are dark, the irides of its eyes are pearl color; but when the pinions are white, the irides are red. Some of these birds are ornamented with a tuft of feathers rising from the back part of the crown of the head.

THE TURBIT.

This variety is somewhat larger than the Jacobin. Its head is round, and beak short; from the breast grows a tuft of feathers named the "purle," spreading in opposite directions, like the frill of a shirt; and from the beak to the purle reaches the gullet.

The colors of this pigeon are mostly yellow, dun, red, blue, and black; and accasionally chequered. According to the fancy, the back of the wings and tail should correspond in color, except in the yellow and red birds, whose tails should be white. A stripe of black should cross the wings of the blue birds, but the other body and flight feathers should be white; they are termed "black-shouldered," or "blue-shoul-dered," as their color may be; and when of one color only,

THE TURBIT.

these pigeons have been sold as "owls." Turbits are also chosen for the shortness of their beaks, and their spreading "purle;" and if well-trained, when young, they will become excellent flyers.

THE NUN.

The nun is greatly admired, from the elegantly contrasting colors of its plumage. Its body is generally white, and its tail and six flight feathers of its wings should be either wholly red, vivid yellow, or black, as likewise its head, which is adorned and nearly covered by a tuft, or "veil," of pure white feathers.

According to its colors, the bird is termed a red, yellow or black-headed "nun," as it may happen to be; and whenever the feathers vary from this rule, the bird is termed "foul-headed," or "foul-flighted," and is greatly diminished in value; but with such as frequently rear clean-feathered birds, as perfect

specimens, it is scarcely possible to obtain one entirely free
from foul feathers. Smallness of head and beak, a pearl eye,
and largeness of veil, are desirable properties in this bird.

THE HELMET.

This variety is a somewhat larger bird than the nun. Its
head, tail, and flight are mostly of one color, either yellow,
blue, or black tint, and the other parts of the body are generally
white; its head bears a delicate tuft of feathers, differing in
color from the body, and in form like a helmet. It is a pretty
bird, but is not a fine flyer. It is most useful as a nurse.

To the varieties already enumerated, I might add several
others, as the "owl," the "ruff," the "spot," the "lace," the
"finnikin," and the "Friezland runt;" but these breeds are not
common, nor are they generally held of much account. As
for the French, Leghorn and the Spanish "runts," they are not
to be placed among the fancy varieties, being remarkable
merely for their size, and are appropiate for the dove cot.

FOOD.

In a state of nature, the rock dove feeds on grain and seeds
of various kinds, as well as on vegetables. According to
Montagu, it also devours some kinds of snails, and is particularly fond of the Helix virgata.

In a state of confinement or *familiarisation*, these birds are
fond of almost every kind of grain, but old tares are found, by
experience, to be the best for them; horse beans, particularly
the smaller sorts, as small ticks, are considered next to tares in
point of nutritive properties; oats, barley, wheat, and peas,
may be given occasionally, and will be found wholesome
varieties of diet. Pigeons are very fond of rape, hemp and
Canary seeds, which, however, should only be given occasionally; and new tares should especially be given to young birds
very sparingly. Many fanciers make a composition of salt,

lime mortar, and a little clay, mixed with spicy seeds, as caraway, which they allow their pigeons to feed upon at will.

The seed may be scattered on the floor amongst the gravel, although many persons recommend little contrivances to put it in, on the score of keeping it cleaner and better.

DOMESTIC ACCOMMODATION AND MANAGEMENT.

FAMILIARISED, or fancy pigeons are generally confined in aviaries, or lodged in appropriate buildings attached to or near the house of the breeder, in order that they may be regularly and easily fed, cleansed, and duly attended to in all matters having reference to their condition and health; for their natural instinct and feeling of liberty have been so nearly effaced, or placed in abeyance by the captivity to which they have been subjected, for so many generations, that they have become nearly dependent upon man for support, and have lost the power or capability, even when allowed to fly at large, of looking for and finding their own food.

In these buildings, it is common to erect a certain number of boxes, or divisions, against the walls or sides, each calculated to accommodate a pair of pigeons, with their nest and young. They succeed best when separate and distinct from each other, with a small platform, and an entrance just large enough to admit the bird; as when disposed in a continuous row, and open in front, they are apt to interfere with each other, and, by their jealousies and contentions, prevent the due increase of eggs and young.

The most common shape for a pigeon house is the one represented in the succeeding illustration, but the form is immaterial. It is, however, necessary that the holes should be large enough for the birds to turn round in with ease; and there should be in front shelves and partitions of from seven to nine inches in depth, so as to keep the couples apart, and afford them resting places; and two holes for each couple, between each partition, will be desirable. The cot should be fixed where it will be

screened from cold winds, which are extremely prejudicial to
the birds; a southern or south-western aspect should, therefore,
if possible, be chosen; visits from cats and rats must also be
carefully guarded against.

PIGEON HOUSE.

If the young fancier be enabled to fit up a loft over a stable,
or other out-building, for a pigeon house, the best arrangement

PIGEON LOFT.

he can adopt is that shown in the above illustration. The
means for exit and re-entrance must be first thought of; and
if there be no window in the loft, two holes must be made in
the wall, at about five feet from the floor, each sufficiently
large to admit a pigeon easily; a shelf should be fastened on
the inside, and another on the outside, of the said apertures; on

this latter shelf, a trap, or "aerie," should be affixed, the intent and purposes of which I shall presently explain. At the upper part of the loft, rough branches should be placed as perches in the manner shown in the representation. At about four feet from the floor, breeding boxes, according to the number of birds intended to be kept, should be securely fixed to the wall, care being taken to protect them from rats, &c.

Some fanciers furnish their boxes with little earthenware pans, or small baskets, for the birds to deposit their eggs in; although the eggs are not so likely to be broken in the baskets as in the pans, the latter, if supplied with straw, are cleaner than the baskets; the pans should vary in dimensions, according to the class of pigeon for which they are designed. It is well to put two of these receptacles in each little room, as the hens frequently go to the nest again when their broods are about three weeks old, leaving them to the care of their mates. Instead of egg boxes, shelves partitioned off, and having sliding fronts for the convenience of cleaning, are used; if the young fancier intend to keep "pouters," the shelves should be fourteen inches in breadth, and at least twenty inches apart, so that the birds may not acquire the habit of stooping, which depreciates their value.

As pigeons drink differently from most other birds, that is, by taking a long-continued draught, like cattle, a fountain, or large-bottomed glass bottle, with a tolerably long neck, for water, should be provided for their house; it should be placed on a small three-legged stool, so that its mouth may incline into an earthenware pan, into which the water will trickle slowly, and cease when it reaches the level of the mouth of the bottle, and a continued supply of fresh water thus be kept up; two or three bricks will serve instead of a stool, to give the bottle the necessary elevation.

To insure the thriving of the birds, the loft and shelves should be kept clean, and gravel strown on the floor; indeed, gravel must on no account be omitted, as pigeons are exceedingly fond of pecking it.

The "aërie" before mentioned, which is fastened on the

shelf outside of the loft, is a trap made of laths. It has two sides and a front only, the wall of the loft forming the back; the front and sides act upon hinges, so that they may be thrown

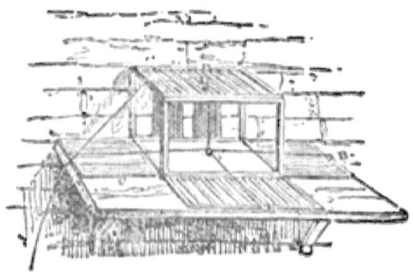

AERIE OPEN.

open, and laid flat on the platform, as in the above figure *A*, *B*, *C*, and on the upper parts of these flaps are fastened strings, united to a single string in the middle of the trap; the string is carried over the swivel *E*, at the top of the machine, to a hiding place, whence the owner can see all that passes, and when a bird alights within the aërie, he jerks the string, the flaps are elevated, and the bird is immediately a prisoner. The aërie, when shut, presents the appearance shown in the following illustration. This kind of trap is used not only by

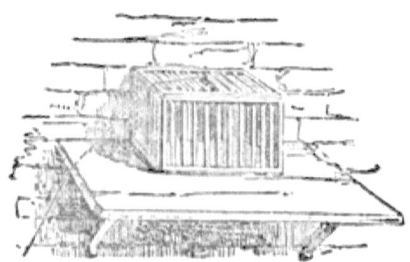

AERIE CLOSED.

fanciers, but by amateurs; and is an important appendage to the loft, both as a means of self-defence to secure strays and to shut in their own birds. Among amateur fanciers, the first-mentioned purpose is to secure valuable and favorite breeds from being deteriorated through stray birds of no value pairing with them. When any strays are taken in the trap, they are killed for the table, unless called for and claimed by their owners, within twenty-four hours after their capture, and a trifling sum may then be demanded for trappage.

To ensure the purity of any particular kind, the young males, as soon as they show symptoms of maturity, which may be known by particular gesticulations and their cooing notes, are placed apart in a chamber appropriated for the purpose, with a female of the same variety. Here they remain till a mutual attachment has taken place, after which, they may be returned to the general aviary, or dove house; for, when once an alliance is effected, it generally continues undissolved and inviolate till the death or removal of one of the parties; on which account many different varieties may be kept in the same aviary, or associated together in one building, without much apprehension of having a contaminated breed.

For mating, or coupling pigeons, it is a good plan to build two cots, divided only by a lath partition, by which means the birds will see each other, and may feed out of the same little vessels; when, by giving them plenty of hemp seed, they will soon be fit for mating. When the hen sweeps her tail, put her in the cock's pen, and they will readily agree. Where it is not convenient to make this probationary pen, and you are obliged to place them both in one coop, put the cock in a few days before his mate, that he may get accustomed to it, and feel himself master, especially if the hen be high spirited; else they will quarrel so fiercely, that their disputes will terminate in a total dislike to one another.

When the pigeons are comfortably matched, allow them the full run of the loft, to select a nest for themselves; or choose a nest for them, and inclose them in it for several days, by means of a slight lath railing, giving them an abundant supply of food and water during the whole time. Both male and female engage in the construction of the nest, and relieve each other in the task of incubation. Two eggs only are laid, and the young are hatched blind, naked, and helpless, and sedulously fed and cherished by both parents. Several pairs of young are reared during the season. The young are fed for some days after exclusion from the egg, not on grain, nor insects, but upon a peculiar lacteous secretion, or curd-like matter, which is poured out from a series of glands in the crop both of the male and female, which glands develope themselves into activity by a mysterious law at the proper juncture. This lacteous fluid is very abundant, and will frequently drip from the bills of the pigeons as they approach their young. It is thrown into the open mouths of the nestlings by a kind of exgurgitation, the receiving one and the giver being both in agitation. In the course of a few days, pulse or grain, moistened in the crops of the parents and mixed with this lacteous curdy fluid, is given, the secretion gradually decreasing as it is less and less required, till at length peas, moistened or macerated in the crop, are alone transferred into those of the young.

About the third day, some of the ordinary food, after maceration in the crop, is added, its proportion being increased, till at length, when the young quit the nest, it constitutes their food entirely.

Though fancy pigeons are kept for the sake of their beauty and peculiarities, the ordinary dove-house pigeon is reared almost exclusively for the sake of its flesh, which is accounted in most countries a delicacy. But how far the rearing of great numbers of these birds is profitable in our country may admit of question; the quantity of peas, beans, and grain, which even a small flock will annually consume, is enormous. What, then, must be the consumption of flocks of many hundreds?

DISEASES.

THE *megrims*, or epilepsy, is an incurable disorder, in which the pigeon moves about and flutters at random, with its head turned, and its bill resting upon its back.

If the birds suffer much while *moulting*, remove them to a

warm place, mix a good quantity of hemp seed in their ordinary food, and tinge their water with saffron.

When the birds are affected with the *wet roup*, give them a few pepper corns once in three or four days, and put some green rue in their water.

The *dry roup* is a husky cough, arising from a cold; when three or four cloves of garlic should be given to the birds daily.

When your pigeons are *infested with insects*, fumigate their feathers thoroughly with tobacco.

The *canker* is occasioned by the cocks pecking each other, which, as they are extremely irritable, they often do. To cure it, rub the part daily with a mixture of burnt alum and honey.

If the incrusted flesh round the eyes of "carriers," "Barbs," or "horsemen," be injured or pecked, bathe it with salt water; and if, in some days, this remedy does not succeed, another lotion composed of three drachms and a half of alum, dissolved in two ounces of water should be tried.

When "pouters" and "croppers" *gorge* themselves, by over-eating, after long fasting, put the bird, feet downward, into a tight stocking, smoothing up the crop so that, overloaded as it is, it may be kept from hanging down; then hitch up the stocking on a nail, and keep the bird a prisoner until its food is digested, supplying it with a small quantity of water occasionally. When the bird is taken out of the stocking, it should be put into an open coop or basket, and fed but scantily for a while.

For *lameness*, or *swelled balls of the feet*, whether from cold, cuts with glass, or any accident, the most effectual application is a small quantity of Venice turpentine spread on a piece of brown paper.

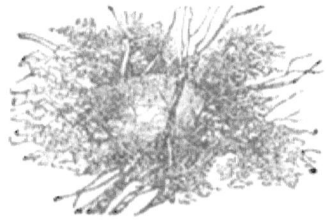

THE EUROPEAN QUAIL.

Synonymes.

Tetrao coturnix,	OF ORNITHOLOGISTS.
Caille,	OF THE FRENCH.
Wachtel,	OF THE GERMANS.
Codorniz,	OF THE SPANIARDS AND PORTUGUESE.
Quaglia,	OF THE ITALIANS.
Quail, Common Quail,	OF THE BRITISH AND ANGLO-AMERICANS.

BESIDES beauty of form and plumage, the song of the common quail of the Old World is no slight recommendation to the amateur. In the breeding season, that of the male commences by repeating softly, tones resembling *verra, verra,* followed by the word *pieveroie,* uttered in a bold tone, with the neck raised, the eyes shut, and the head inclined on one side. Those that repeat the last syllables ten or twelve times, consecutively, are the most esteemed. That of the female only consists of *verra, verra, pupu, pupu,* the last two syllables being those by which the male and the female attract one another's attention; when alarmed or angry, their cry resembles *guillah!* but at other times, it is only a murmur, resembling the purring of a cat. This bird never sings when left to run about in a light room, except during the night, but continually when in a darkened cage.

When wild, the quail is found throughout the eastern continent. It is a bird of passage, arriving in Europe in May, and taking its departure at the end of September.

THE EUROPEAN QUAIL.

FOOD.

In a wild state, the quail feeds on wheat and other corn, rape seed, millet, hemp seed, and the like. It also eats green vegetables, as well as insects, and particularly ants' eggs.

In the house, it is fed on the same food, adding bread, barley meal, mixed with milk, the universal paste, and occasionally salad or cabbage, chopped up small, and, that it may want nothing to keep it in health, plenty of river sand for it to roll in and peck up grains, which assist its digestion; but this sand must be damp, for if dry, it will not touch it. It drinks a great deal, and the water, contrary to the opinion of some persons, should be clear, and never turbid. It moults twice in the year, once in autumn, and again in spring; it then requires river sand, and greater attention than at other times.

BREEDING.

THE quail breeds very late, never before July. Its nest, if it can be called so, is a hole scratched in the earth, in which it lays from ten to fourteen bluish-white eggs, with large brown spots. These are hatched after three weeks' incubation. The young ones, all hairy, follow the mother the moment they leave the shell. Their feathers grow quickly, for in the autumn they are able to depart with her to the southern countries. The males are so ardent, that if one is placed in a room with a female, he will pursue her immediately with extraordinary eagerness, tearing off her feathers if she resist in the least; he is less violent if he has been in the same room with her during the year. The female, in this case, lay a great many eggs but rarely sits on them; yet if young ones are brought her from the field, she eagerly receives them under her wings, and becomes a very affectionate mother to them. The young must be fed on eggs, boiled hard and cut small, but the best way is to take the mother with the convoy, which may be done with a net. She watches over them attentively, and they are more easily reared. During the first year, one would think that all the convoy were females, the males resemble them so much, particularly before the brown shows itself on the throat.

The adult female, however, differs very sensibly from the male; her throat is white, and her breast paler, and spotted with black, like that of the throat.

MANAGEMENT.

IN the house, if allowed to range, its gentleness, neatness, and peculiar motions are seen to advantage; but it is often kept in a cage of the following make:—

A small box, two feet long, one foot deep, and four high, of any shape which is preferred; in this are left two or three openings, one for drinking at, the other to give light; besides this all is dark; the bottom is a drawer, which should be covered with sand, and have a seed drawer at one end; the top is of green cloth; for as the quail often springs up it would hurt itself were it of wood. The case should be suspended during the summer outside the window, for the quail sings much more when confined in this manner than if allowed to range the room, where there are many things to call off its attention from its song.

THE
AMERICAN ROSE CULTURIST;

BEING A

PRACTICAL TREATISE

ON THE

PROPAGATION, CULTIVATION, AND MANAGEMENT

OF

THE ROSE

IN ALL SEASONS; WITH A LIST OF CHOICE AND APPROVED VARIETIES,
ADAPTED TO THE CLIMATE OF THE UNITED STATES.

TO WHICH ARE ADDED

FULL DIRECTIONS FOR THE TREATMENT OF

THE DAHLIA.

Illustrated by Engravings.

'———No flower that blows
like the Rose, nor scatters such perfume "

New-York:
ORANGE JUDD COMPANY, 245 BROADWAY.

THE

AMERICAN

BIRD FANCIER.

NEW-YORK:

ORANGE JUDD COMPANY,

No. 245 BROADWAY.

Winter Greeneries
AT HOME.

By Rev. E. A. JOHNSON, D. D

Author of " Half Hour Studies of Life," etc., etc.

This Volume differs from most other works on winter gardening, in giving
the results of actual practice. The author for several years past has found re-
creation in beautifying his study with plants; his work has resulted in so
much enjoyment to himself and his friends that he has been induced to tell
what he did, and how he did it. The book is not a mere dry set of directions,
but its teachings are presented in the pleasant form of letters to some young
ladies, who, having witnessed the author's success, have asked his instruction,
and this allows a genial personality to pervade the work, and makes it withal
readable, as well as instructive. It is a most excellent guide to successful win
ter-gardening, as suited to American homes, with our peculiar domestic sur-
roundings, and those who follow its teachings will reach a satisfactory measure
of success. The engravings include several representations of the author's study

FINELY ILLUSTRATED. 12mo. PRICE, POST-PAID. $1.

ORANGE JUDD COMPANY, 245 Broadway, New York.